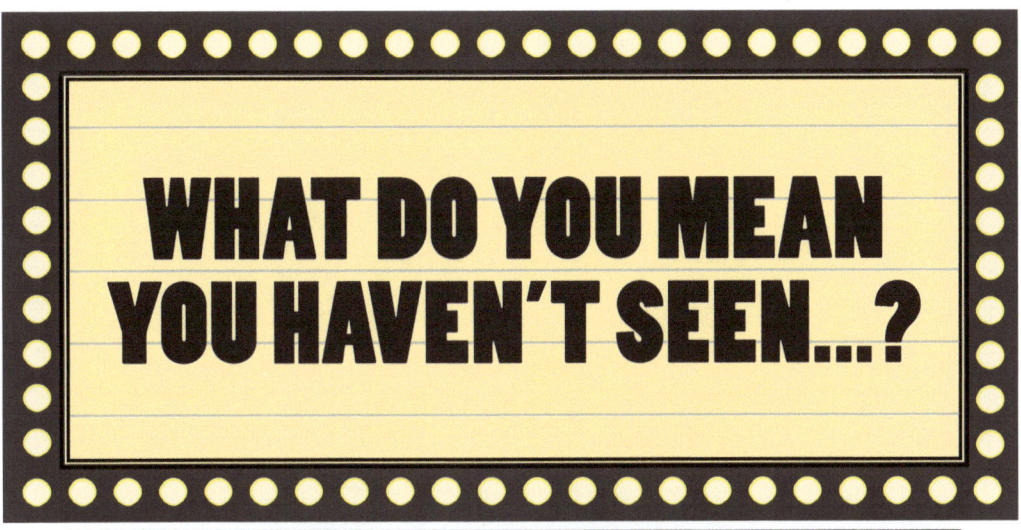

*A Family Guide to Classic Movies*

by K.C. Brown

© Copyright 2007, 2009 Normandy Press, All rights reserved.
Normandy Press, 1616 Eleventh Ave. W., Seattle WA 98119

www.normandypress.net

ISBN-13: 978-0615563824

*For Craig Wilson, a good
friend and a good man,
whose Video Isle is the place
where our family most loves
to be cast away*

# contents

Introduction.................4
Using this book..............5

## JANUARY
The Court Jester.............6
Duck Soup....................7
Singin' in the Rain..........9
The Flame and the Arrow.....10

## FEBRUARY
Stormy Weather..............11
Sabrina.....................13
The Wizard of Oz............15
Bringing Up Baby............17

## MARCH
High Noon...................18
The Quiet Man...............20
It Happened One Night.......22
Seven Brides for Seven Brothers....24
Harvey......................26

## APRIL
Easter Parade...............28
The Defiant Ones............30
Animated Film Night.........32
Viva Las Vegas..............34

## MAY
On the Waterfront...........35
Mary Poppins................37
I Remember Mama.............39
The Guns of Navarone........41
Witness for the Prosecution.....43

## JUNE
High Society................45
Adam's Rib *or* Pat and Mike....47
Life with Father............49
Dr. No......................51

## JULY
Yankee Doodle Dandy.........53
Shane.......................55
Some Like It Hot............57
Bridge on the River Kwai....59

## AUGUST
Silent Movie Night (The Great Clowns)..61
The Sound of Music..........64
Casablanca..................66
A Hard Day's Night *and* Help!....68
To Kill a Mockingbird.......70

## SEPTEMBER
My Fair Lady................72
Rebel Without a Cause.......74
The Treasure of the Sierra Madre....76
The Ladykillers.............78

## OCTOBER
Sullivan's Travels..........80
The Taming of the Shrew.....82
Frankenstein *and* Bride of Frankenstein....84
Abbott and Costello Meet Frankenstein....86

## NOVEMBER
Mr. Smith Goes to Washington....87
The African Queen...........89
To Catch a Thief............91
Top Hat.....................93
Lawrence of Arabia..........95

## DECEMBER
A Tree Grows in Brooklyn....98
It's a Wonderful Life......100
A Christmas Carol (Scrooge)....102
White Christmas............104

Acknowledgments............106
Coming Attractions.........107

# introduction

"What do you mean, you haven't seen...?" That cry punctuated the early years of my marriage as my husband, aghast at each new revelation of some gap in my film-viewing history, took charge of my movie education.

He spent the '50s in Akron, Ohio, watching double features at the movie theater every Friday, Saturday and Sunday. And the early '60s chasing down every important new release and art house foreign film in Pittsburgh, Hartford, New York and Paris. (At the time, I was just getting started on *Bambi* – so I had a lot of catching up to do.)

As we continued watching movies together, and our laps started to sprout children, we realized that we could share our affection for the great classic movies with our kids. Before 1968 there was no Motion Picture Association rating system for films. Why? Because it wasn't needed. The Production Code (also known as the Hays Code) had been in effect in Hollywood since 1934, requiring a degree of self-censorship by directors and studios. Sex and violence might be hinted at offscreen – but it was very rare for anything graphic to be shown. And the movies that lasted did so because they depended not on sensationalism or special effects, but rather on cracking good stories and memorable performances. There were fewer screens available then, but families were welcome at all of them.

When you send your kids to school, you expect them to come out with at least a nodding acquaintance with the must-read books in our culture. If you provide them with a religious education, you expect them to become familiar with the Bible, the Torah, the Koran or other great spiritual texts. But who will introduce your children to The Medium of the Twentieth Century (the medium to which America has made such a great contribution)? No one but you.

If you've seen *The Wizard of Oz* with them, and you probably have, your kids will catch any references to the Scarecrow, the Tin Man and the Cowardly Lion. But popular culture is full of references to movies that, increasingly, your kids won't have watched. If they've never heard Marlon Brando holler "Stellllaaaa!" or mutter "I coulda been a contender," or seen the Marx Brothers try to cram a dozen people into a ship's stateroom, they're missing some of the common currency of American culture. And as we fail to pass on these great film experiences, the gap between the generations widens, and the kids' historical awareness dates only to the latest Disney comedy.

This book is designed to help you with this great project of transmission of culture...in the form of a year's worth of thoroughly enjoyable Saturday nights at the movies with your family. If you are an adult using this guide to help fill some gaps in your own film-viewing history, we urge you to watch all these excellent movies as soon as possible. Then you too can start annoying your friends with the cry, "What do you *mean* you haven't seen....?"

# using this book

Do you have to watch the movies in order? Of course not. Watch them any time you choose, as the mood strikes you. Just bear in mind that the year's recommendations are front-loaded with some of the most accessible, easy-to-fall-in-love-with movies in the early months, and more challenging films introduced as the year progresses.

We've mixed up the genres and styles, and made some seasonally appropriate choices. Since we live in Seattle, a steady diet of black and white classics in the winter, juxtaposed with the grey skies outside, would be a recipe for a serious case of seasonal affective disorder. On the other hand, a moody, rain-slicked film noir can be just the ticket after a long hot summer day at the beach.

Some younger people balk at watching movies in black and white. If that happens, go back to the Marx Brothers and try again. We have introduced the black and white choices gradually. Once your children get used to them, and get to know some of the stars, you will hear them saying "Oh, there's Cary Grant!" rather than "How come it's not in color?"

For each month we offer 4 or 5 suggestions, since the availability of the films may vary (as well as the number of weeks). We don't provide a full plot synopsis of each movie – that would ruin half the fun. But we do offer a personal take (no bones about it) on what makes the movie worth watching, special moments to watch for, perspective on the performers, sometimes context for the movie and cross-references to other great films and performances.

You will not find a certain number of stars assigned to a movie, like a restaurant guide. This is not a book of criticism. If a movie is here in these pages, it's because we have watched it with our children, we all loved it and we think you will too. And because if you want to be "in the know," some of the greatest images and performances in popular culture are right here to be enjoyed.

**Age Appropriateness.** You are the best judge of what your child is ready for. When appropriate, we will offer a word on "The Tricky Bits" – moments or thematic elements that may get parents wincing, or cause children to ask difficult questions. Some of these would be awkward for one family, but comfortable for another, and most provide opportunities for "teachable moments." Movies made before 1968 would all rate what would now be a G or, at most, PG rating, so you are not going to be blindsided by inappropriate language or gore (this is more than I can say for network television today). Tricky Bits are more likely to be reminders of less enlightened times, like African-Americans relegated to playing the maid or manservant, or attitudes about gender which we now find outdated.

**Attention Span.** Again, you know best what your kids are capable of. Many of these stories are told so compellingly that 90 minutes fly by without a fidget. Some of these films are longer, but we have found our kids equally engaged. Just be prepared when you are about to watch an epic. Have snacks handy, hit "Pause" and take a break when needed, or even view a film over several nights.

**Black & White.** For kids accustomed to visual overload, black and white films can take some getting used to. Resist the urge to rush out and find a colorized version, though (they often wind up unintentionally making the movie look cheap). Many of the re-mastered and reissued versions are superb in quality. Ultimately, the black and white liberates the imagination – like great radio drama.

**Aren't we supposed to limit screen time to 30 minutes a day?** This is a common piece of advice to parents – and if we are talking about kids watching screens that flash rapid-fire images at them, with commercial messages and a restless, aggressive visual style, it seems like excellent advice. In fact, 30 minutes a day of that kind of stuff may be too much. Both of us are theater professionals, so we've always felt that characters speaking dialogue, and engaged in interesting action, represent a pretty fine way to tell a story to kids. This is especially true in the period before kids become ready to listen to chapter books – when their attention span for listening or reading is not yet very long. This is the age at which our kids started to watch 90-minute films – not frantically paced, but simply engaging stories well told. They are now both avid and accomplished readers, and the stories that were "told" them in the movies have only deepened their skills as interpreters of story, theme and character.

**Why isn't my favorite movie included?** There are so many wonderful movies, we couldn't fit them all in this first volume of *What Do You Mean You Haven't Seen...!* In each case, we had to consider not only the greatness of the movie, but its accessibility and appropriateness for family viewing. *Citizen Kane*, for example, tops many lists of "greatest film ever made" but it is not the easiest evening for younger kids to enjoy. *Gone with the Wind* is just plain looooong. Others are paced too fast (*His Girl Friday*) or too slow (*Stagecoach*), or offer characters who are a little too sinister (*Rear Window*) or strange (*Sunset Boulevard*). Our aim is to help our children (and ourselves) develop a taste for the classics…an appetite for the more challenging ones should develop naturally.

Once you fall in love with these movies, though, watch for our recommendations for the next year of viewing: *What Do You Mean You Haven't Seen...? Build Your Own Film Festival*. One of our greatest pleasures has been to take a favorite performer and explore his or her versatility. Our own family "Jimmy Stewart festival" featured a week or more of westerns, comedies, dramas and adventure movies with this remarkable actor. At other times we have binged on Fred Astaire or the Marx Brothers, or gone from one great musical to another. This follow-up guide will allow you to go deeper into any genre you were drawn to, or to follow the individual careers of these great performers or directors.

But what are we waiting for? Break out the popcorn….. it's movie night!

## JANUARY
### COMEDY/MUSICAL

# The Court Jester

*1956, 101 minutes, color*

**Featuring Danny Kaye, Glynis Johns, Basil Rathbone, Angela Lansbury, John Carradine.** *Written and directed by Melvin Frank and Norman Panama*

Has there ever been an entertainer more charming than Danny Kaye? Fans of his more sentimental side can check out his portrayal of Hans Christian Andersen, in the 1952 film of the same name. But for an evening of adventure spoof that crackles with wit, nothing can beat *The Court Jester*.

Danny Kaye plays Hubert Hawkins, a former circus performer who has joined a band of Robin Hood-style outlaws in the woods led by 'The Black Fox.' He goes undercover as a court jester in the castle of a king who has usurped the throne from the royal family. There he meets, and pretends to work for, Basil Rathbone and his treacherous lords (one of their interchanges has become a watchword in our house: "Get it?" "Got it." "Good.") His 'captain' in the Black Fox band is Maid Jean, played by the lovely Glynis Johns, who later in her career appeared as Mrs. Banks, the suffragette mother in *Mary Poppins*.

*The Court Jester* is famous for the tongue-twisting scene just before the joust: "The pellet with the poison's in the flagon with the dragon; the chalice from the palace has the brew that is true." Equally delightful is the high-speed knighting scene, and the song 'The Maladjusted Jester' with lyrics by Sylvia Fine (Kaye's wife, who wrote much of his material throughout his career).

Perhaps the highlight, though, is the scene in which Kaye is enchanted by a sorceress and starts switching from coward to swashbuckler, literally at the snap of a finger. Apparently only Basil Rathbone's real skill as a fencer protected him from some of Danny Kaye's derring-do with a sword during some takes. The movie is brim-full of comedy, adventure and romance – and features a young Angela Lansbury in an ingénue role (a treat for those who know her best from the TV series *Murder, She Wrote*).

> *"The pellet with the poison's in the flagon with the dragon; the chalice from the palace has the brew that is true."*

## JANUARY
### COMEDY/MUSICAL

# Duck Soup

*1933, 68 minutes, black-and-white*

**Featuring Groucho, Chico, Harpo and Zeppo Marx, Margaret Dumont, Louis Calhern.** *Directed by Leo McCarey, story by Bert Kalmar and Harry Ruby*

What is the best way to meet the Marx Brothers? As quickly as possible. One could debate for hours which is the best of their movies, or which is the best one to start with. But since each of their films features anarchy, fun and zany shenanigans, just pick one, dive in and get to know the brothers.

For the sake of argument we are suggesting *Duck Soup* because it is fairly short and features all four of the performing brothers (a fifth, Gummo, was part of their earlier vaudeville act on stage, but never appeared on screen). Many consider *Duck Soup* to have the greatest LPM (laughs per minute) of the Marx Brothers films. It also omits the standard interludes in which Chico plays the piano and Harpo plays the harp – which either enrich the films or slow down the stories, depending on your perspective.

The opening of the film may not seem geared to children, as it features a group of stuffed shirt politicians considering the future of their little kingdom of Freedonia, which is on the verge of bankruptcy. The rich widow Mrs. Teasdale (played by the Marx Brothers' irreplaceable straight-woman, Margaret Dumont) will only agree to write another large check to keep the country afloat if they install her candidate, Rufus T. Firefly, as president. Don't worry…it is only moments before Groucho, as Firefly, makes his entrance sliding down a fireman's pole and the antics begin. No politician has ever outdone Groucho's promise, couched in a bouncy song and dance number, "If you think this country's bad off now, just wait till I get through with it!"

Having been introduced to Groucho's trademark sardonic wit and rubber-limbed dance moves, and Zeppo's young leading man voice and bearing, we are now ready to meet the remaining anarchists in the bunch. Playing Chicolini and Pinky, spies for the neighboring country of Sylvania, are Chico (prounounced "Chicko" in honor of his fondness for the ladies) with his amiably fake Italian accent and his broad charm, and curly-wigged Harpo, whose only 'voice' is a horn and who leaves a path of seemingly innocent destruction wherever he goes. In one classic scene, the two torment a street vendor with a lemonade cart, and include a beautiful example of vaudeville hat business.

The boys are always ready to be a nuisance to authority figures, including Ambassador Trentino of Sylvania, who hired them. The great character actor Louis Calhern provides the appropriate indignation as Harpo snips off his tie and imports chaos into his office. (Years later, at the end of his career, Calhern lent his considerable dignity to the role of Uncle Willie in *High Society* – but this time as a man who has seen so many high-jinks in his day, he is immune to shock, or even willing to shock others.)

In another famous scene, Harpo dresses like Rufus T. Firefly and pretends to be his mirror image – which almost

> *"If you think this country's bad off now – just wait till I get through with it."*

works, until a third Firefly appears (Chico). (Harpo reprised the mirror routine many years later with Lucille Ball on her television show.)

The final scene is a fantastic free-for-all, which can be seen as an indictment of the madness of war throughout history. Firefly appears in a different costume in each sequence, and the exterior of the building in which the brothers are holding off a siege has a tendency to morph into different locations. The Marx Brothers might have downplayed the political message of the film in favor of the fun, but were nevertheless delighted when Mussolini took it personally enough to forbid *Duck Soup* to be shown in Italy.

**NEW PARLOR GAME:**

A great character deserves a great entrance, and Groucho's entrance as Rufus T. Firefly is one of the best. The band gives him a fanfare, and we fully expect him to enter between the line of assembled dancers. No dice. Then another fanfare, with even greater expectation. Meanwhile, Groucho slides down a fire-pole and appears at one side, with the assembled audience awaiting the great Firefly. Not only is this a great trickster gag, it plays with our expectation that a major character will be given a great entrance.

We started watching how different movies set up the entrance of a major character. In many cases, the more important the character, the more the director backs off and waits, to build anticipation. Think of the first time we see James Bond on screen in *Dr. No*: not only do we have to wait for the character to be introduced, but at first we only get to see his hands at the baccarat table, and to hear the famous line in voiceover: "The name is Bond. James Bond." Or think of Spencer Tracy's character in *Pat and Mike*, who doesn't appear in the first few scenes (even though we are perfectly aware this is a Hepburn-Tracy vehicle). How does he make his long-anticipated entrance? Climbing through a window into Katharine Hepburn's room. You can have a lot of fun watching for the innovative, and sometimes impish, ways that film-makers will present their major characters' first entrance.

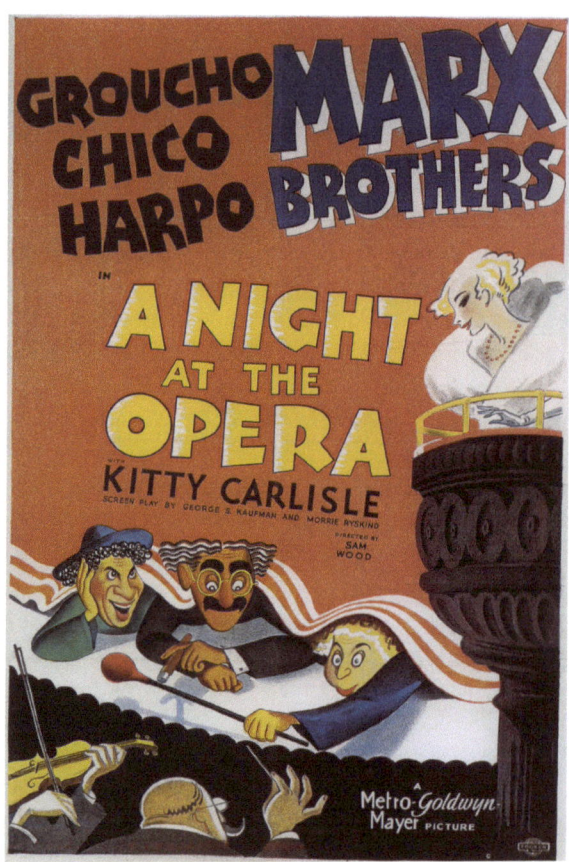

**TRICKY BIT:**

Sharp eyes may recognize that the scene in which the legislature of Freedonia debates whether to go to war breaks into a musical number which equates nationalism with a minstrel show. At the time the film was made, there was not yet a feeling of discomfort and distaste for minstrel shows in themselves. And the Marx Brothers were ahead of their time in being staunch supporters of the rights and dignity of African-American performers.

## JANUARY
### COMEDY/MUSICAL/ROMANCE

# Singin' in the Rain

*1952, 103 minutes, color and b&w*

**Featuring Gene Kelly, Donald O'Connor, Debbie Reynolds, Jean Hagen, with appearances by Cyd Charisse and Rita Moreno.** *Directed by Stanley Donen and Gene Kelly, written by Betty Comden and Adolph Green*

Even people who don't like musicals love this one. And it contains one of the ultimate 'what do you mean you haven't seen' moments: Gene Kelly splashing through the rain singing that oh-so-catchy title song. The story makes hay with Hollywood's transition from silent movies to talkies. Gene Kelly plays Don Lockwood, an aspiring song and dance man, whose star suddenly rises when he is romantically paired in films with screen goddess Lina Lamont. The year is 1927 and Al Jolson's 'The Jazz Singer' has just come out and created a sensation – so all the studios are racing to bring out their own talking pictures. Not every performer in the silent era made a successful transition to the talkies, a fact that *Singin' in the Rain* fully exploits. (This fact was explored in a darker vein in Billy Wilder's masterly *Sunset Boulevard*.)

Sound technology is fairly new, which makes for some hilarious scenes on the set, as actors and technicians struggle to film the new Lamont-Lockwood movie 'The Dueling Cavalier.' But the greatest challenge is Lina's shrieky, nasal voice, which threatens to ruin the picture. In a memorable moment she manages to make her character, despite the full powdered wig and 18th century dress, sound like a gum-popping New Jersey waitress ("I caaaaan't staaand 'im"). Jean Hagen plays the gorgeous, clueless blonde with great aplomb, and practically runs away with the movie. (She was nominated for the Academy Award for Best Supporting Actress.) Playing dumb convincingly is harder than it looks, and is often accomplished by very intelligent actresses like Judy Holliday, for whom the role was originally written. The producers decided that, after her huge success in 'Born Yesterday' on Broadway, she wouldn't be interested in a supporting role – so they turned to Jean Hagen, her understudy.

'The Dueling Cavalier' is saved by dubbing Lina Lamont's disaster of a voice. Don Lockwood has discovered, and fallen for, an unknown actress named Kathy Selden, played by a young Debbie Reynolds, and he gets her the job of replacing Lina's voice without the star's knowledge. Needless to say, the studio also decides to capitalize on Lockwood's (or Kelly's) assets, and the film becomes 'The Dancing Cavalier.' Gene Kelly gets several notable 'character dances' with partners like Rita Moreno and Cyd Charisse (with whom he was later paired in *Brigadoon*). However the most spectacular number, in a movie filled with great dancing, is performed by comic sidekick Donald O'Connor. In 'Make 'em Laugh,' a celebration of the lengths to which an old vaudevillian will go to entertain us, we see O'Connor literally climbing the walls. Gene Kelly was famous for his virile, athletic style of dancing – but here O'Connor outpaces him with sheer acrobatic brio.

*Singin' in the Rain* is full of fond, mocking references to earlier films and Hollywood figures. However, you don't need any of this insider trivia to thoroughly enjoy the film. It balances romance and humor with one knock-out musical/dance number after another. One small piece of trivia, though, is worth a smile. Jean Hagen in reality had a beautiful, rich voice. When we hear the dubbed voice of Lina Lamont in 'The Dancing Cavalier' it is not Debbie Reynolds's voice we hear – it is Jean Hagen, speaking for herself.

## JANUARY
### ADVENTURE

# The Flame and the Arrow

*1950, 88 minutes, color*

**Featuring Burt Lancaster, Virginia Mayo, Robert Douglas, Aline MacMahon, Frank Allenby.** *Directed by Jacques Tourneur, written by Waldo Salt*

The region of Lombardy (in Italy) in the Middle Ages sounds at first like the setting for a dry historical epic…but think Robin Hood. And think Burt Lancaster, with his million-dollar smile, charming the ladies as an untamed mountain man (and a dead shot as an archer), who lives to resist the tyranny of the German conquerer Count Ulrich (known as 'The Hawk'). Lancaster plays Dardo Bartoli, and this swashbuckler allows him full rein for the skills he learned in his earlier career – as a circus performer. He is joined here by his good friend and former partner Nick Cravat as Piccolo (the character name may allude to his short stature: 5'4"). The two were paired in several films, but Cravat was cast here (and in *The Crimson Pirate*) as a mute character, apparently because of the thick Brooklyn accent he was unable to lose, even when wearing tights or pirate breeches.

Dardo's complaint against Count Ulrich is as much personal as political. Ulrich stole his wife and, early in the movie, goes on to capture his son. The main action of the movie is devoted to Dardo's attempt to steal his son back, while the proud Anne de Hesse (played by Virginia Mayo) first disdains him and then, of course, falls meltingly in love with him. There is a spicy scene in the woods where Anne, as Dardo's captive, asks to bathe in the lake - while he literally keeps her on a rope. Her attempt to trick Dardo is, needless to say, thwarted by his quick wits and distrust of women…and they prove themselves a match for one another.

Romance, swordplay and acrobatics – fortunately this is a genre that delivers up many pleasures and thrills, without taking itself very seriously at any point. The big payoff here is when Dardo and Piccolo make their way into Count Ulrich's castle disguised as acrobat/entertainers and have to deliver some real acrobatic stunts. As they stand on one another's shoulders or walk a tightrope high over the great hall, you can see the incredible skill and mutual trust that made them a successful acrobatic team. The explosion of hold-your-breath stunts and swordplay looks very much like what *The Court Jester* is sending up in its climactic scenes in the castle hall and on the battlements.

If your taste runs more to sun-bronzed pirates than men in tights, you can find the same concoction of romance and bravura stunts in *The Crimson Pirate* (1950, 105 minutes, directed by Robert Siodmak and co-produced by Burt Lancaster). Again we have rebellion against tyranny – although the original screenplay by Waldo Salt, who wrote *The Flame and the Arrow*, was scuttled by the studio, because of anxieties about his left-leaning tendencies. (In 1951, Salt refused to testify before the House Committee on Un-American Activities and was blacklisted. Years later, after the blacklist was history, he came back to win Academy Awards for writing *Midnight Cowboy* and *Coming Home*.)

*The big payoff here is when Dardo and Piccolo make their way into Count Ulrich's castle disguised as acrobat/entertainers and have to deliver some real acrobatic stunts.*

## FEBRUARY
MUSICAL

# Stormy Weather

*1943, 78 minutes, black-and-white*

**Featuring Bill "Bojangles" Robinson, Lena Horne, Cab Calloway, Katherine Dunham, Fats Waller, Fayard and Harold Nicholas, Ada Brown, Eddie "Rochester" Anderson, Dooley Wilson.** *Directed by Andrew L. Stone, story by Jerry Horwin, screenplay by Frederick J. Jackson*

One of the best ways to make a musical that doesn't strain credulity is to tell a story about characters who happen to be entertainers. That way they can burst into song, or dance on a table, and no one thinks anything of it. Fred Astaire used the device to great effect in one movie after another. *Stormy Weather* takes this successful formula one step further and includes not just one or two stars but an entire company of the top African-American performers of the mid-20th century, in one jam-packed extravaganza of incredible talent. A paper-thin romantic plot allows time for over 20 musical numbers and a couple of great comic turns in a mere 78-minute running time. There could be no better way to celebrate Black History Month than by getting to know this exceptional group of performers.

Morgan Freeman has argued against observing Black History Month, on the grounds that the history of African-Americans and the history of the United States are indivisible. That may be true, but you would never know it from watching *Stormy Weather*. At the time it was made, there was practically absolute segregation between black entertainers and the white entertainment industry. Bill "Bojangles" Robinson danced from the age of 6 in the black theater circuit that nurtured so many talented performers, and did not appear before a white audience until he was 50 years old. Once he started being cast in films with white performers, he tended to play the butler who mentored a young Shirley Temple with some dance moves. Lena Horne, beautiful, glamorous and talented, was given stand-alone musical numbers that could be cut out without disturbing the plot when the movies were shown in the South. Only in the all-black world shown in *Stormy Weather* (and *Cabin in the Sky*, a successful Broadway musical also made into a film in 1943) could Lena Horne be the leading lady she was born to be.

The story is loosely based on Bill Robinson's life (and similar to that of some of his contemporaries). After serving in the First World War in a black regiment nicknamed "The Harlem Hellfighters," he returned and began to truly make his mark as a dancer. Robinson's character, named Bill Williamson for the film, woos a beautiful singer by the name of Selina Rogers – but this romance is not drawn from Robinson's actual life. It gives *Stormy Weather* a classic shape – boy meets girl, boy loses girl, boy gets girl – and offers Lena Horne a leading romantic role as Selina. And it serves its purpose, despite a lack of on-screen chemistry between the two stars. Robinson was 65 at the time the film was made, and Horne was some forty years his junior. Perhaps more importantly Ms. Horne, who became a strong advocate for the rights of African-American performers, apparently harbored private feelings that Bill Robinson was a bit of an Uncle Tom. Whatever choices Bill "Bojangles" Robinson made in order to secure the progress of his career, there is no question he influenced many 'hoofers' with his loose-limbed 'copacetic' style (he apparently coined the word) and was greatly admired by Fred Astaire among many others.

Highlights are plentiful in this movie. They include the legendary Fats Waller at the piano, singing "Ain't Misbehavin'." This was his last screen appearance; five

*An entire company of the top African-American performers of the mid-20th century, in one jam-packed extravaganza of incredible talent.*

months after *Stormy Weather* opened he died, of pneumonia, at the age of 39.  Another legend on view is Cab Calloway, fronting his band in a zoot suit with his signature high-energy dance moves, singing "hep, hep."  Dooley Wilson (the piano player Sam in *Casablanca*) provides a comic foil as Bill Williamson's chronically broke but endlessly resourceful friend Gabe Tucker.  Lena Horne sings the famous title song *Stormy Weather* with support from the dancers of Katherine Dunham's company.  Dunham, a pioneer whose African-American dance company endured for 30 years, combined her anthropological interest with the black folk culture of different countries with the newly emerging styles of modern dance.

Even in a musical that moves from strength to strength there has to be one show-stopper, and fortunately (or sensibly) it comes near the end.  The Nicholas Brothers performing "Jumpin' Jive" is an absolute knock-out – Astaire called it the best musical sequence ever filmed.  What is known as the Harlem Renaissance, in which black musical theater, blues and jazz were so important, launched Fayard and Harold Nicholas, a spectacular "flash dancing" team, as children - in careers that lasted until the 1990s.  You will be hard pressed to keep from "ooh-ing" and "aah-ing" aloud as you watch them literally leap-frog over one another down a large staircase, each one landing in a full split and then drawing himself up to a stand again without using his hands.  This dazzling number was shot in one take, and it showcases not only the musicality and upbeat energy, but the most astonishing athleticism one could ever hope to see in a pair of dancers.  Mikhail Baryshnikov was a fan as was Gregory Hines, a major figure in the resurgence of tap dancing late in the 20th century.  Hines claimed that if the story of the Nicholas Brothers were ever filmed, their dance numbers would have to be achieved with digital help, because no dancer alive could actually duplicate them.

Remarkably, 1943 saw the production of a second major African-American musical, *Cabin in the Sky*, directed by Vincente Minnelli at the start of his career (before going on to *Meet Me in St. Louis, An American in Paris, Brigadoon, Gigi* and marriage to Judy Garland).  Based on a successful Broadway musical, the story features the forces of Lucifer trying to win the soul of "Little Joe" Jackson (played by Eddie Anderson, who was Jack Benny's "Rochester") from his good and loving wife Petunia, the immortal Ethel Waters.  The temptress Georgia Brown was played by Katherine Dunham on stage; in the movie the part went to Lena Horne.  Louis Armstrong also has a featured role, and Duke Ellington and his orchestra have a musical number.  For a while the movie was frowned on because it featured the familiar sight of singin', dancin' Negroes, and did not offer a picture of the social realities faced by the African-American community.  But this was an unfair task to lay at the doorstep of a story that is simply a fable, nothing more, nothing less.  It would be like complaining that *The Wizard of Oz* doesn't provide a searching portrait of the realities of the Depression in the Midwest.  *Cabin in the Sky* offers angels and devils, music and romance, and a showcase for the talents of an exceptional cast – what more could one ask?

# FEBRUARY
### COMEDY/ROMANCE

# Sabrina

*1954, 113 minutes, black-and-white*

**Featuring Humphrey Bogart, Audrey Hepburn, William Holden, John Williams, Walter Hampden.** *Directed by Billy Wilder, screenplay by Billy Wilder, based on a play by Samuel A. Taylor*

February is the month of Valentine's Day and it is time to fall in love – with Audrey Hepburn. "Once upon a time, in a house on Long Island Sound" is the narration we hear at the beginning of *Sabrina*. It is Hepburn's voice, and a fitting way to begin what is essentially a Cinderella story (one of her specialties). The camera soon picks up Sabrina, perched in a tree…the chauffeur's daughter looking in on a party at the mansion. Beguilingly lovely in every role she played, Audrey Hepburn is here paired with not one, but two leading men who can hold their own with her. William Holden plays David Larrabee, a son of the wealthy family and a charming bounder, whom Sabrina has loved since childhood. Humphrey Bogart is his brother Linus: the serious, sober and responsible son who looks after the Larrabee family's multiple business concerns.

The domestic staff are concerned about Sabrina's lifelong fascination with David, feeling that she is "reaching for the moon." In particular her father, Fairchild the chauffeur, displays a kind of reverse snobbism about it, believing that it's not good for the classes to mingle too freely. So he dispatches Sabrina to cooking school in Paris, hoping to apply a geographical cure. Needless to say, Fairchild's plan backfires. Sabrina leaves Long Island a shy young girl with a pony tail (an older gentleman who takes Sabrina under his wing in Paris announces, "You must stop looking like a horse!") She returns transformed, with a very becoming short haircut, a stunning wardrobe, and the confident air of a woman of the world. She is unrecognizable, but certainly no longer invisible to David, who is completely captivated by the grown-up Sabrina. As, indeed, who could fail to be? All the elements that make up Audrey Hepburn's unique appeal are present in *Sabrina*: the freshness that never seems forced or put on, the dancer's grace, the slight carefulness in her speech pattern which reflects her blue-blood Dutch and English heritage, and the insouciant charm with which she wears the stylish clothes designed for her by Hubert de Givenchy.

Speaking of charm, William Holden has it in spades here, as the ne'er-do-well ladies' man David. One cannot help liking him, even as one earnestly roots for him *not* to get the girl. Our hopes ride on Linus, as the romantic underdog, played delightfully against type by Humphrey Bogart. (The role was originally intended for Cary Grant.) We are accustomed to thinking of Bogey as the hardboiled detective, the tough guy with the cigarette in one corner of his mouth. Sabrina exploits the warm, devoted heart underneath…which gave those tough guys their depth and complexity. In order to protect David's engagement to a young lady whose family represents a major business deal for the Larrabees, Linus takes on the assignment of diverting Sabrina from her infatuation with his brother. Picture Humphrey Bogart preparing for a romantic sailing trip by getting his old Yale sweater out of the closet as he deadpans "Boola boola."

*Sabrina* is a fairy tale with a happy ending to warm any romantic's heart. But it is a fairy tale served with a slice of wry. This is largely thanks to director Billy Wilder, who also helped adapt the screenplay from Samuel Taylor's play *Sabrina Fair*. Billy Wilder was one of Nazi Germany's many gifts to America: he escaped from Europe and made his way to Hollywood in 1933, bringing with him a wealth of experience as a screenwriter in the sophisticated entertainment scenes of Vienna and Berlin. It was not long before Wilder was writing in English with wit and brio, and he continued writing screenplays throughout his

*Sabrina is a fairy tale with a happy ending to warm any romantic's heart. But it is a fairy tale served with a slice of wry.*

distinguished directing career. Darker films like *Double Indemnity, The Lost Weekend* and *Sunset Boulevard* were balanced with sparkling comedies like *Ninotchka, The Seven Year Itch* and *Some Like It Hot*. Wilder's films were noted for strong dialogue and for the performances he got from actors (*Sabrina* is only one of the times he used William Holden to great effect). Never has the classic struggle of brother against brother yielded more guilty pleasure. And watch for the running gag of champagne glasses slipped into one's trouser pockets…the payoff, at the Larrabee patriarch's expense, will make you wince with laughter.

## FEBRUARY
FANTASY/MUSICAL

# The Wizard of Oz

*1939, 112 (101) minutes, b&w and color*

**Featuring Judy Garland, Frank Morgan, Ray Bolger, Bert Lahr, Jack Haley, Billie Burke, Margaret Hamilton.**
*Directed by Victor Fleming, adapted by Noel Langley from a novel by L. Frank Baum*

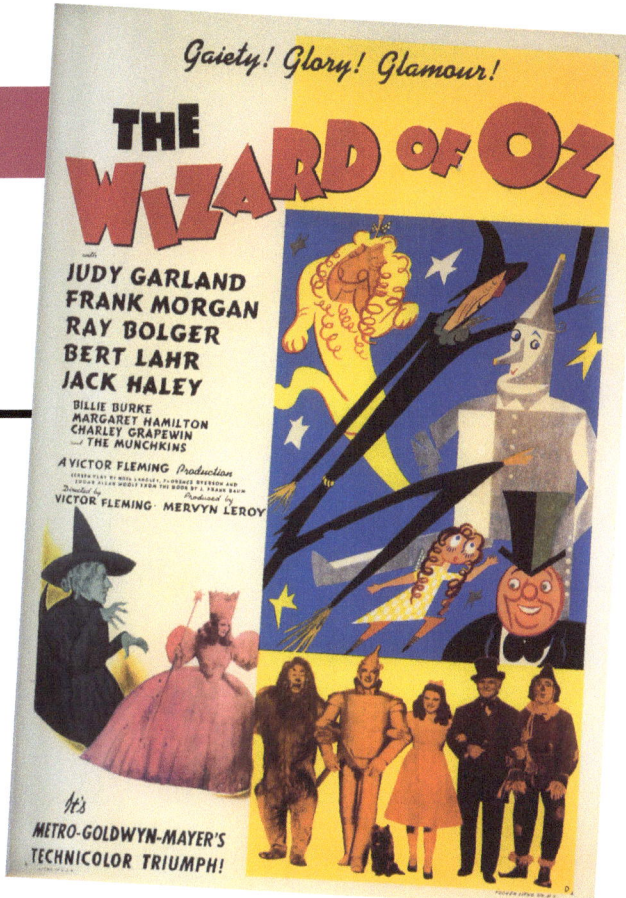

This is the ultimate "What do you mean you haven't seen - ?" movie. If, by chance, you are one of the few people who have missed *The Wizard of Oz*, you have missed some of the most indelible film images in our collective consciousness, and you owe it to yourself to correct the situation immediately. If, like so many people, you saw it as a child (or with your children), you still owe it to yourself to give it another, perhaps a closer, look. This film endures as a classic because it offers many satisfactions, on many levels.

There is the story, in which the archetypal fairy tale elements of witches, the dark forest, the challenging journey, are rendered with the high gloss of 1930's movie musical style. This alchemy has been much imitated, but has rarely been so successful. There are the memorable songs by Harold Arlen and Yip Harburg (the iconic 'Somewhere Over the Rainbow' was almost edited out of the film, because it was felt that it didn't advance the plot). For children, *The Wizard of Oz* is likely to become an essential part of their inner imaginative landscape. For adults, there are many other reasons to revisit the film.

Lovers of Hollywood can savor the incredible moment where the film shifts from sepia toned (the world of reality in Kansas) to color (the magical realm of Oz). This was the year that color technology was first introduced to the movies, and the film deftly capitalizes on the transition to the tools newly available to them. It is a pleasure, too, to see Judy Garland at a time when her star was just rising and she was not yet suffering from the heartache and addiction of later years (some blamed the producers of this film for starting their teenage star on various drugs, to keep her on track with their grueling shooting schedule).

One can also savor the performances of the vaudeville song-and-dance men recruited for the silver screen to play Dorothy's companions. Ray Bolger (the Scarecrow) was an old hoofer, as was Jack Haley (the Tin Man – listen for his trace of a Boston accent). Bert Lahr, as the Cowardly Lion, imported his signature 'nnnnnggggg' from his own vaudeville act. Bert's son John Lahr, a theater critic, claimed that his father was too big for the movie screen, so he could only make it in Hollywood playing an animal.

If you are interested in the social overtones of the film, watch for how the hardworking, grey life of Aunt Em and Uncle Henry's Depression-era farm is contrasted with the bright world of fantasy offered by Hollywood and Broadway. The Oz novels, written by L. Frank Baum, contain a deep critique of the American economic system. It is said that the city of Oz was named for 'oz.' – the abbreviation for an ounce of gold. The Wizard as confidence man was his dig at the financial wizards who pulled strings behind the scenes as America was growing.

And finally, let's return to that word 'archetype,' and consider a Jungian psychology perspective on the film. We were concerned that our 18-month-old wanted to watch *The Wizard of Oz* again and again, and asked a psychologist friend whether this was okay. His answer was, "Well, it's a little bit early, but the movie is there inside him already." What did he mean? That Dorothy's adventure is a journey of individuation, which every young person must eventually undertake, from the safety

*For children, **The Wizard of Oz** is likely to become an essential part of their inner imaginative landscape.*

of home and family to the dangerous state of individuality and maturity. The four companions (Dorothy, the Scarecrow, the Tin Man and the Cowardly Lion) form an archetype of wholeness – representing self, mind, heart and courage. Toto represents Dorothy's animal nature, while the threatening forces in Oz are her shadow, the aspects she must overcome and master, and finally draw strength from. When she returns from her 'dream' journey and all the challenges she has faced, she is able to embrace her home and the familiar characters there as a whole, contented person.

Sound like too much? Well, maybe so. Just relax and enjoy the film anyway. It's probably all there inside you.

*This film endures as a classic because it offers many satisfactions, on many levels.*

# FEBRUARY
### COMEDY/ROMANCE

## Bringing Up Baby

*1938, 102 minutes, black-and-white*

**Featuring Katharine Hepburn, Cary Grant, Charlie Ruggles, May Robson, Walter Catlett, Barry Fitzgerald.** *Directed by Howard Hawks, screenplay by Dudley Nichols and Hagar Wilde*

Bringing Up Baby is now widely considered one of the funniest screwball comedies of all time. Its original audience wasn't quite ready for it. It was a box office failure, possibly for the same reason it is so loved now: the relentlessly madcap action and non-stop witty dialogue. Howard Hawks, the director, was fired from his next project for the studio and Katharine Hepburn had to buy out her studio contract and endure the label "box office poison." Yet today this film consistently ranks on lists of the top movies ever made. (It also continues to provide income for Hepburn's estate, as she was an investor in the film.)

Cary Grant plays against type here, abandoning the debonair lady's man he played to perfection in so many films. Here he fashions a beautiful characterization of a bumbling paleontologist, David Huxley, who seems destined for a life of piecing together dinosaur bones and is headed for a loveless marriage to a waspish assistant. He meets his nemesis, however, in the figure of Katharine Hepburn's socialite Susan Vance, who cheerfully derails his plans and drags him into one farcical situation after another. Susan is keeping company with a real leopard, named 'Baby,' sent by her brother in Brazil, to be delivered to her millionaire aunt. Needless to say, the only way to keep the leopard calm is to sing to it 'I can't give you anything but love, Baby.'

As David Huxley's life spins out of control, the couple find themselves on their way to deliver Baby to Susan's wealthy aunt in Connecticut. Add in a circus leopard who looks just like Baby but is not the least bit tame, a dog who discovers and buries the priceless 'intercostal clavicle' dinosaur bone David has been seeking, and a night in the county jail – and you get a sense of the non-stop predicaments in which the characters find themselves.

This was Katharine Hepburn's first outing in comedy, and she lacked the ease and impeccable timing that Cary Grant had in such abundance. A number of old vaudevillians were engaged to help her find her comic feet, the most successful of these being Walter Catlett, playing the town constable. Hepburn enjoyed working with him so much that she asked for his part to be expanded, so he could spend more time on set and with her.

It is believed that Cary Grant's characterization in *Bringing Up Baby* is based on the work of silent film star Harold Lloyd. Indeed, Grant's physical performance here is worthy of one of the great silent screen clowns, with pratfalls and acrobatic moves performed without benefit of stunt double.

### TRICKY BIT:

At one moment Susan, who is falling for David and does not want him to leave her aunt's home, contrives to conceal his clothes and leave him stuck wearing a distinctly feminine negligee. When another character asks why he is wearing it, Cary Grant departed from the script and ad-libbed his own line: "Because I just went gay all of a sudden." The word 'gay' was not in common usage at the time to signify 'homosexual.' Mr. Grant's awareness of that world has been speculated about, but at this time it would have seemed not only an innocent but actually a baffling thing to say. (All the same, this moment was edited out of television showings of the movie for years!)

## MARCH
#### WESTERN

# High Noon

*1952, 85 minutes, black-and-white*

**Featuring Gary Cooper, Grace Kelly, Thomas Mitchell, Lloyd Bridges, Katy Jurado, Otto Kruger, Lon Chaney Jr., Lee Van Cleef.** *Directed by Fred Zinnemann, written by Carl Foreman, based on a story by John Cunningham*

Frank Miller is coming back to town – and that's not good. Five years ago Marshall Will Kane arrested him for murder, and the judge sent him to jail. But he's managed to get an early release, and he's coming back to exact his revenge. Three of his tough buddies are waiting for him at the little train station, and he is due in at high noon.

So begins another classic, and one of the greatest westerns ever made. *High Noon* is not one of the shoot-'em-up cowboys 'n' Indians kind of films we often think of when the word 'western' is mentioned. It is a taut psychological thriller about a man who really ought to save his own skin in the face of a threat, but who can't because it's not in his character to run from danger or to back down from doing what's right. Gary Cooper won an Academy Award for Best Actor for his performance as Marshall Kane. It was a comeback movie for Cooper – and what a comeback. "Coop" had been a major movie star since the 1930s, but his career had cooled for a few years before he was offered this role. Marshall Kane became not only a defining performance for him but a potent image of the lone man standing up for what's right.

The film opens with Dimitri Tiomkin's haunting theme song, "Do Not Forsake Me, O My Darlin'," sung by Tex Ritter with a throbbing accompaniment that sounds like an anxious heartbeat. Marshall Kane has just married Amy Fowler, a young Quaker woman (played by a dewy Grace Kelly). They are set to leave town and start a new life elsewhere, although one can tell it is a little hard for him to finally hand over his badge. Just as the couple is about to leave town, the news comes of Frank Miller's imminent return. The 85-minute running time of the movie almost parallels the time remaining until high noon, and the recurring shots of clocks ticking away the intervening minutes keep the tension wound tight throughout. The new sheriff isn't due to arrive until the next day, so Kane decides he needs to stay.

Kane figures that the townsfolk will remember the lawlessness that prevailed when Frank Miller was free, and will rally to fight his return. He figures wrong. The judge who sentenced Miller is only too happy to pack his bags and flee, and the best support Kane finds anywhere in town is the advice that he do the same. As we watch an increasingly isolated man walk the streets of his town looking in vain for help, we are invited to think of the fear and paranoia that prevailed during the tenure of the House Un-American Activities Committee. (Screenwriter Carl Foreman was called to testify before the Committee during the production of *High Noon* and, refusing to name names, was blacklisted and unable to work in Hollywood for years, although he established a successful career in England.) Another indelible image of menace which recurs in the film is the train tracks stretching into the distance, from which the danger will arrive. Events in Europe during the Second World War may have been on the mind of director Fred Zinnemann. An Austrian-born Jew, he had worked with Billy Wilder in Europe before coming to America in 1930.

Zinnemann had an extraordinary career spanning many decades, and is said to have cited the three most

> *Marshall Kane became not only a defining performance for Gary Cooper but a potent image of the lone man standing up for what's right.*

important factors in making a good film as "the script, the script, the script." Perhaps he did not give himself enough credit, because he had exceptional success in eliciting great performances from actors. Gary Cooper's acting was famously considered somewhat 'flat' by people who would watch him on set. But when his performance was seen on screen it was clear that the camera had reached in and found a powerful intensity within his understated approach. Zinnemann's casting of Grace Kelly as Marshall Kane's bride, twenty years his junior and a staunch pacifist, launched her career. She went on to become a screen goddess and the Princess of Monaco, but here she is just a clear-eyed professional, holding her own with some great screen performers. These include Lon Chaney, Jr. playing, as he did in *The Defiant Ones* and as the Wolfman, a basically decent man trying to leave behind a dangerous past. Lloyd Bridges is featured as the callow deputy who resents not having been entrusted with the sheriff's badge. Thomas Mitchell as the Mayor and Lee Van Cleef as one of Miller's gang are familiar, and always reliable, performers. Katy Jurado is a less typical Western figure. Dark-eyed women of easy virtue and Latina-sounding spitfires are a staple. But Jurado was a well-known Mexican actress; her accent in the movie is real. As Helen Ramirez, the saloon owner who once loved Will Kane, she sees clearly what is going on in the town and, with her great dignity and presence, anchors the moral center of the story.

It is part of our expectations in a classic western that the good guys should ultimately win. *High Noon* is, all the same, a story of disillusionment. Will Kane does the right thing, but he learns that the people he most thought he could count on are capable of turning their backs – and the person he least expected to pick up a weapon is the one who saves his life. The star he had been so reluctant to shed is tossed in the dust, as we are left to wonder: we count on our heroes, but what happens if they can't count on us?

## MARCH

**DRAMA/ROMANCE/COMEDY**

# The Quiet Man

*1952, 129 minutes, color*

**Featuring John Wayne, Maureen O'Hara, Barry Fitzgerald, Ward Bond, Victor McLaglen.** *Directed by John Ford, story by Maurice Walsh and screenplay by Frank S. Nugent*

If the month of March puts you in mind of wearing green and yearning for the Emerald Isle, there is no better time to screen *The Quiet Man*. It is also a great opportunity to see John Wayne in a role that doesn't require cowboy boots or a Marine uniform. Wayne plays Sean Thornton, an American boxer who is traumatized by accidentally killing an opponent in the ring. He escapes his nightmare by going to Ireland to reclaim his family's farm. There he meets and falls in love with Mary Kate Danaher, played by the beautiful Maureen O'Hara. Mary Kate is the quintessential Irish redhead, with a fiery temperament to match. Their courtship is orchestrated and watched over, in accordance with old custom, by the priest and the local matchmaker – to the bemusement of Wayne's impatient American.

Many of the customs he encounters in Ireland strike Sean Thornton as more baffling than quaint. Not the least is the fact that, because he disapproves of the match, Mary Kate's brother "Red" Will Danaher refuses to provide her with her rightful dowry. Mary Kate cannot feel like a properly married woman without her "treasure" and demands that Sean take her brother on, man to man, before she will behave like a wife. There is a delicious tension in watching John Wayne resist being urged to "fight like a man" – no one in Ireland knows of Thornton's past, and his troubled relationship with fighting. When he finally is provoked beyond restraint by Victor McLaglen's bull moose Danaher, the fight that breaks out is an epic donnybrook (and a very funny one), with the combatants fighting their way across fields and through streams and haystacks, urged on by an ever-growing crowd of townsfolk. Needless to say, Mary Kate's honor (and the Thorntons' domestic harmony) is restored.

Ireland has never looked more beautiful than in this film's lush Technicolor cinematography, which won an Oscar. Another Oscar went to John Ford for his direction: one of the four he won in his career, the most of any director in Academy history. John Ford typically made lean, muscular Westerns, and he was a director's director. He rarely shot more than a couple of takes, and virtually edited the film in the camera by getting exactly the shots he wanted, just the way he wanted them. John Wayne had acquired the rights in 1933 for the story on which *The Quiet Man* is based (reportedly for $10). Wayne and John Ford and Maureen O'Hara apparently made a handshake agreement in 1944 to make the film together. But there were very few producers willing to gamble on an Irish story that looked as though it wouldn't make any money. Republic Pictures agreed to make it only on condition that Wayne and Ford and O'Hara would make a western for them first, to offset their anticipated losses. They did – *Rio Grande* in 1950 – and then finally got to film their little Irish piece...which garnered 7 Academy Award nominations and turned out to be a huge financial success for Republic.

*Ireland has never looked more beautiful than in this film's lush Technicolor cinematography, which won an Oscar.*

### TRICKY BIT:

The Irish are portrayed here very much as our clichés would have them: provincial, bound by tradition, and devoted to drinking and fighting. That being said, the film showcases many famous Irish theater actors of the time, and is one of the rare movies in which authentic Gaelic can be heard spoken on screen.

There is a suggestion that the stubbornness of Maureen O'Hara's feisty Irish colleen is answered by John Wayne's character with something that looks a lot like domestic violence. There is a lot to talk about here, too, about whether we can truly understand what constitutes honor for a woman in a different culture. That is one achievement of the movie, that the ways of the Irish are presented to us as every bit as unique and foreign as they appear to Sean Thornton.

If *The Quiet Man* is too salty for the very young children in the house, and you still want to introduce them to all the images of Ireland that form part of our cultural storehouse, try *Darby O'Gill and the Little People* (Disney, 1959, 93 minutes). Here they will find lilting accents, drinkers and brawlers, dreamers and storytellers, leprechauns and banshees…and, best of all, a young Sean Connery as a local swain (his performance in this film helped him win the role of James Bond). It is a pleasant hour and a half, and features enough Irish blarney to fill a box of Lucky Charms.

## MARCH

**COMEDY/ROMANCE**

# It Happened One Night

*1934, 105 minutes, black-and-white*

**Featuring Clark Gable, Claudette Colbert, Walter Connolly, Roscoe Karns, Jameson Thomas.** *Directed by Frank Capra, story by Samuel Hopkins Adams, screenplay by Robert Riskin*

This movie surprised quite a few people when it came out – in particular its stars, Clark Gable and Claudette Colbert. Several other A-list stars had turned down the lead roles, and these two were stuck with the movie, for one reason and another. They both thought they were making a turkey. After the shoot, Claudette Colbert was on her way out of town on a train, declining to make an appearance at the Academy Awards ceremony. Imagine her surprise when the producers sent someone to pull her off the train to come and accept her Best Actress Oscar – along with the Best Actor, Best Director, Best Screenplay and Best Picture awards the movie picked up. It was the first, and last, movie to sweep the Oscars this way until grand slams for *One Flew Over the Cuckoo's Nest* in 1975 and *The Silence of the Lambs* in 1991.

We were surprised, too, when we watched the film with our children. Black and white, 1934, a little over an hour and a half...and the kids loved it so much they insisted it go into the book. What is the appeal? And why is it so surprising?

*It Happened One Night* is sometimes referred to as the first screwball comedy. It has many of the elements which became essential to the genre. There is a spoiled heiress and a regular fellow who brings her down to earth. They "meet cute," meaning they don't much like one another at first, and then gradually fall in love. They are mismatched, but thrown together on a road trip – call it the first road movie or buddy movie. In short, the movie is everything that was later imitated, played upon, referred to, "quoted", satirized and paid homage. On its own, without all those echoes, it is simply a great story, well told, about characters one is delighted to get to know. Dialogue and dilemma are not presented at breakneck comic speed, but rather at a gentle pace that anyone can follow and enjoy.

Clark Gable plays Peter Warne, a newspaperman who is being fired on the telephone by his New York editor – but somehow lets all the friends who are eavesdropping outside the phone booth imagine that he is quitting. Claudette Colbert plays Ellie Andrews, a rich young woman who has been sheltered by her overprotective father to the point where she has become petulant and spoiled. She has impulsively married a celebrity aviator named King Westley, just to escape her father's protective net. But her father has scooped her up after the ceremony, before the couple could have a moment together, and is trying to arrange for an annulment. Ellie escapes by diving off her father's yacht moored in Florida, and finds her way to a night bus to New York, to rejoin King Westley.

Of course, she meets Clark Gable on the bus. He likes to crack wise, but he is easily detected as one of nature's gentlemen. One cannot quite tell whether it is his instincts as a reporter, or as a knight in shining armor, which cause him to see through Ellie's petulance. But it is not long before he is protecting her from herself and her innocence. Whatever is meant to have happened 'one night' actually happens over several nights, in which he chivalrously arranges for humble lodgings for her, as their travel plans go awry. On the first night a bridge on their route is washed out – and he arranges for them to share a rented cabin. He divides the room with a blanket strung between the two beds, but when Ellie is slow to duck over

> *Sometimes referred to as the first screwball comedy, it has many of the elements which became essential to the genre.*

to her side of the blanket, Warne starts to undress. Apparently this scene was too cumbersome to shoot, with the dialogue, when Gable had to remove his tie, shirt and undershirt. So the undershirt was dispensed with. He removed his shirt, showed his handsome bare torso – and across the country sales of undershirts plummeted after the movie opened.

Pretty tame by today's standards, but much tension is achieved by the notion of the two attractive stars sleeping chastely on either side of a suspended blanket, known in the film as "the walls of Jericho." On the second night that their travel plans are derailed, they find themselves sleeping under a pair of haystack, and Warne scavenges a bunch of carrots for his hungry (and ungrateful) charge. Here is a treat for cartoon fans. Chomping carrots while he talks, threatening a fast-talking fellow traveler with a fictional gangster named "Bugs Dooley"…it turns out that Clark Gable is one of the inspirations for Bugs Bunny!

This is not, however, the achievement for which we chiefly remember Mr. Gable. He was known as The King of Hollywood. He was paired with every major leading lady including, most famously, his performance as Scarlett O'Hara's love Rhett Butler in *Gone With the Wind*. This was a full five years after he gave a famous lesson to Claudette Colbert in how to hitchhike, using various ways to waggle your thumb at a driver. Colbert was a legendary leading lady in her own right, and used to drive cameramen crazy, insisting that she only be photographed from her right side – her "better" side, as she thought. One of the high points of *It Happened One Night* comes when Colbert's character decides to show Gable's how to hitch a ride by hitching one's skirt. Movie history… your children will love it.

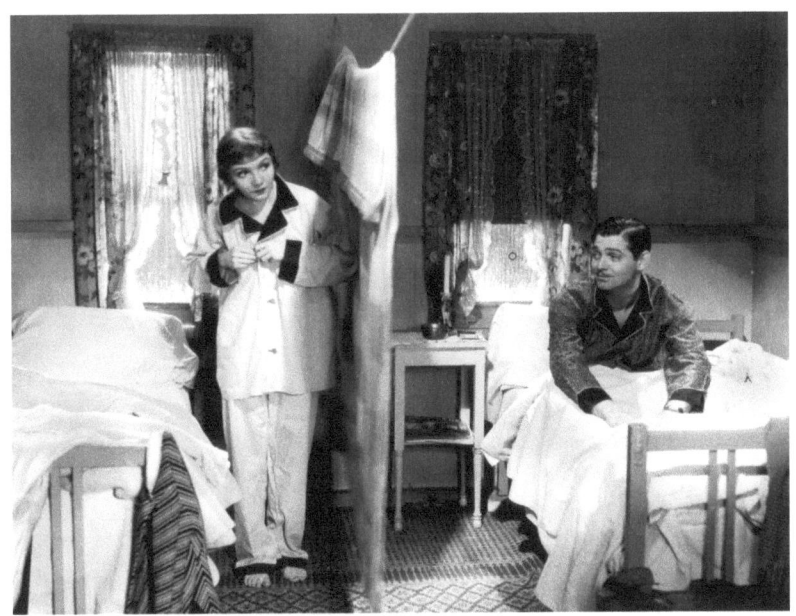

*Director Frank Capra*

## MARCH

### MUSICAL/ROMANCE/COMEDY

# Seven Brides for Seven Brothers

*1954, 102 minutes, color*

**Featuring Howard Keel, Jane Powell, Jeff Richards, Russ Tamblyn, Tommy Rall, Matt Mattox, Marc Platt, Jacques D'Amboise.** *Directed by Stanley Donen, written by Albert Hackett, Frances Goodrich and Dorothy Kingsley, based on a story by Stephen Vincent Benet, music by Gene De Paul, lyrics by Johnny Mercer*

With all the great American musicals that have made their way from Broadway to the silver screen (*Oklahoma, Carousel, Showboat, The Music Man, The King and I*, to name but a few), why single out *Seven Brides for Seven Brothers*? We could tell you that the reason is it is one of those rare musicals that made the opposite journey: conceived and created specifically as a movie, only later to find a life on stage. But that's not really it. We just simply love it, that's all. It has entertained our kids since they were little, and at the ages of 8 and 14 they continue to get unalloyed pleasure from watching it (so do we). At 102 minutes, it is shorter than many of the big name musicals mentioned above – and for color, slapstick and lively fun it is unbeatable.

The story is set in 1850 in the Oregon Territory, so it has a western/pioneer ambience. It opens with homesteader Adam Pontipee, just in town for the day to trade beaver pelts for some molasses, some chewing tobacco, some farm gear – and a wife. Adam is a determined man, and he has the advantage of being played by tall, strapping Howard Keel (sometimes referred to as the John Wayne of musicals, with a dash of Clark Gable and Errol Flynn). In his buckskin jacket, with his manly bass-baritone on display, singing "Bless your beautiful hide, wherever you may be," he is indeed a tempting catch. Or so thinks Milly (Jane Powell), who falls for him at first sight. Powell, a coloratura soprano, can match Keel note for note, and has some sass as well – to complement her wholesome, girl next door quality (she played Fred Astaire's sister and dancing partner in *Royal Wedding*). Life is tough on the frontier and there's little time for old-fashioned courting, so the two pay a visit to the preacher and are on their way back to the Pontipee farm before the day is out.

The trouble is that Adam has neglected to mention to Milly that he shares the farm with six brothers – six rough, unwashed, uncouth and uncivilized brothers. Milly discovers that instead of a romantic idyll, she has signed on for a huge clean-up operation…think Snow White and the seven dwarves. Being a good frontierswoman, she rolls up her sleeves and gets not only the house but the Pontipee brothers in order. In a bit of Biblical whimsy, their parents had been working their way through the alphabet in naming them: Adam, Benjamin, Caleb, Daniel, Ephraim, Frank (who is teased about his name being short for 'Frankincense') and Gideon. It turns out that the younger brothers polish up quite nicely and quickly become a fine-looking set of red-haired fellows, ready to learn the art of courting and winning brides for themselves.

Their chance to meet some local girls comes at a barn-raising, and it is our chance to see one of the most dazzling dance numbers ever filmed. Choreographer Michael Kidd knew that the idea of backwoodsmen suddenly getting up to dance could be laughable, so their moves are sometimes folksy, sometimes athletic, always virile and fresh. They engage in a dance-off with the men from town, stealing their partners, challenging them to feats of balance and strength, and showing off their acrobatic prowess. All this with an infectiously lively

> *The star appeal of Howard Keel was at its peak, coming between his appearances in* **Annie Get Your Gun**, **Show Boat** *and* **Kiss Me, Kate**.

version of "Bless Your Beautiful Hide" carrying the action along, as the Pontipee brothers begin to win the girls' hearts – and lose their own. Four of the brothers were cast for their dancing ability and one (Russ Tamblyn as Gideon) because he was a gymnast. Tamblyn, fresh-faced and boyish here as the youngest son, went on to immortality as Riff in *West Side Story*. Howard Keel, of course, is featured as a singer and actor, and we don't see too much dancing from Benjamin (Jeff Richards, a baseball player before he became an actor). What the other brothers have to show for themselves is unforgettable.

The barn-raising scene, which also features a spectacular choreographed fight, is not the only dance highlight of the movie. In the beautiful number "Lonesome Polecat" the love-struck brothers, back on the farm, have to continue their chores. But they haul logs and chop wood in the slow, balletic rhythm of a moony ballad. Songwriter Johnny Mercer contributed words to many beloved hits ("Moon River," "That Old Black Magic," "Ac-Cent-Tchu-Ate the Positive"), and his lyrics for *Seven Brides* often feature a knowing wink and a salty turn of phrase. Apparently the censors were uncomfortable with the line in this song that suggests "A man can't sleep when he sleeps with sheep." But since there were no actual sheep present in the scene at that moment, they let it go.

Mercer's saucy humor also informs "The Sobbin' Women" (the song shares a title with the Stephen Vincent Benet story upon which the movie is based). Books were rare and precious commodities in pioneer times, and Milly has brought two into her married life: the Bible and Plutarch's *Life of Romulus*. It is from this latter classical work that Adam gets an idea, based on the abduction of the Sabine - or sobbin' - women by a group of Roman men. Tired of seeing his brothers moping about, he decides that "taking a bride" is a phrase that should be taken literally. (Kids: do not try this at home. Although bride kidnapping is still practiced in some corners of the world, it is rather frowned upon in technologically advanced Western countries.)

Plutarch was clear that, although the incident is often referred to as "The Rape of the Sabine Women," there was actually no sexual force employed and the women were allowed freedom to choose whether to accept their would-be husbands. And with Milly in charge of the Pontipee household there is no opportunity for hanky-panky either, in spite of the fact that an avalanche causes a dozen love-sick young people to be snowed in all winter. The girls are all played by professional dancers, as we see in the lovely number "They say when you marry in June." A happy ending for the lovers is to be expected, although it is achieved through an unexpected twist. Perhaps the greatest pleasure in watching the film is seeing how boys will be boys – and how much they love it when they fall under the civilizing influence of girls.

The studio did not have high hopes for *Seven Brides for Seven Brothers*, since it was an untested commodity. They were banking on *Brigadoon*, produced the same year, and so they pulled much of the budget director Stanley Donen had been promised. As a result, he had to shoot many scenes in front of painted backdrops instead of on location. However, the co-director of *Singin' in the Rain* was not afraid of artifice. Now it seems no more odd to see the actors on what is clearly a set than it does to see back-woodsmen elevate simple pioneer chores to the level of dance. All sins are forgiven when one gets to enjoy a sophisticated script (Albert Hackett and Frances Goodrich also collaborated on *The Diary of Anne Frank*). The star appeal of Howard Keel was at its peak, coming between his appearances in *Annie Get Your Gun, Show Boat* and *Kiss Me, Kate*. And then those dances... The studio bet wrong: *Brigadoon* was a modest success, but never approached the huge popular appeal of the brothers and their brides.

## MARCH

### COMEDY/DRAMA/FANTASY

# Harvey

*1950, 104 minutes, black-and-white*

**Featuring James Stewart, Josephine Hull, Peggy Dow, Charles Drake, Cecil Kellaway.** *Directed by Henry Koster, written by Mary Chase*

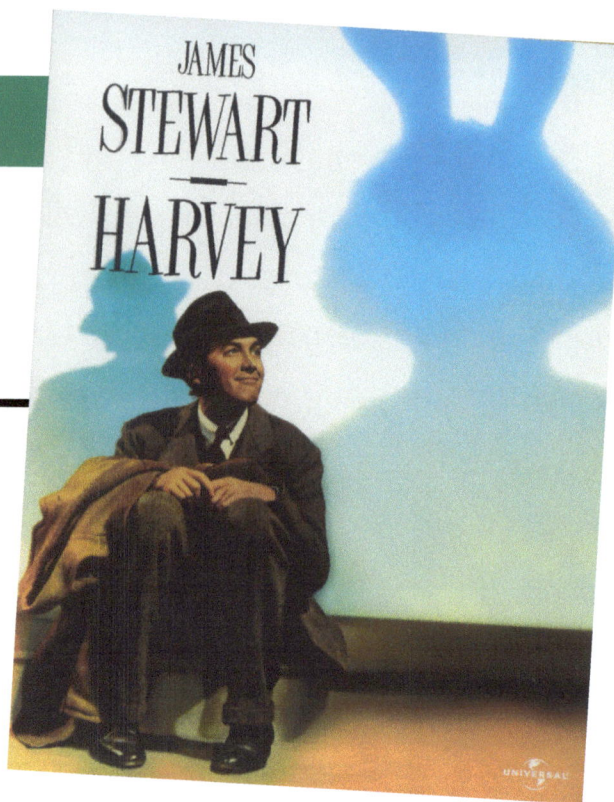

Given the choice, would you rather be smart or pleasant? Elwood P. Dowd has opted for pleasant, much to the consternation of his sister Veta, with whom he shares a home. Veta wants a normal social life and a chance to marry off her daughter, Myrtle Mae. But Elwood insists on handing his card to perfect strangers he happens to meet, and cordially inviting them for dinner. And then, of course, there is his friend Harvey, the six foot three-and-a-half inch invisible rabbit.

Harvey is a Pooka, an animal spirit found in Celtic mythology, mischievous but essentially benign. It is natural to assume, as the story begins, that Elwood's ability to see Harvey is a by-product of his fondness for alcohol or a symptom of a mental disorder. In a fit of frustration, Veta even attempts to have Elwood committed to a mental institution. However, Elwood's innocence and goodness have a protective effect…through a misunderstanding, it is Veta who winds up being committed. By the time the mistake is discovered and almost corrected, Elwood is not the only person who is convinced that Harvey is real.

James Stewart was one of the greatest practitioners of the art of film acting. Without making visible changes to his appearance or personal rhythm, he inhabited his characters with utter conviction. Always psychologically real and believable, Stewart often used his own humble persona to portray an Everyman who was somehow capable of heroic things. In *Mr. Smith Goes to Washington* and *It's a Wonderful Life*, he takes on the forces of corruption and greed, in politics and in business, armed with little more than his deeply held values and unshakable sense of self. One of the very hardest tasks, though, for actors of intelligence and worldly experience is to embody a character who is truly innocent. This is Stewart's achievement in *Harvey*. His Elwood P. Dowd is a man of deep sweetness, not stupid by any means, but rather childlike in his openness to others.

As our 8-year-old daughter pointed out, Elwood "is kind of like a child, because usually it's children who have invisible friends." One might argue as well that children are trusting, content to live in the present and spend time with friends, and able to look past social status to judge whether someone is nice or mean. Elwood's company is particularly enjoyable because he combines the naivete and vulnerability of a child with the perfect manners of a courteous and thoughtful adult. What a contrast we find in Dr. Lyman Sanderson of the sanatorium (played by Charles Drake), who is so focused on his work, his ambition, and his own status that he fails to see the love that is available to him from his lovely assistant Miss Kelly (Peggy Dow). Sanderson is convinced of the importance of being "oh so smart," although a few hours with Elwood Dowd and Harvey go a long way to showing him the value of being "oh so pleasant." Cecil Kellaway, as the director of the institution, also recaptures his own lost innocence and imagination through his encounter with the pooka.

The screenplay of *Harvey* is by Mary Chase, based on her own Pulitzer Prize-winning (and highly popular) play. The play has long been a staple of high school drama departments, perhaps because it addresses questions that all adolescents face: how much ambition should an adult have, and what parts of childhood have to be sacrificed in order to be a successful grownup? The brother and sister,

*It addresses questions that all adolescents face: how much ambition should an adult have, and what parts of childhood have to be sacrificed in order to be a successful grownup?*

Elwood and Veta, were played on Broadway by none other than James Stewart and Josephine Hull, who reprise their roles in the film. Stewart was nominated for the Academy Award for Best Actor, and Hull won as Best Supporting Actress. Hull's Veta is easy to like because she clearly loves her brother. It's just that his eccentricity puts a crimp in her social climbing – and the conflict she feels keeps a constant high-energy fizz in Hull's performance. Veta is a woman on the edge of a tizzy, while Elwood is steadily and quietly unconflicted and comfortable with himself.

Comedy thrives on contrast. Oscar is messy and Felix is meticulous (*The Odd Couple*); Oliver Hardy is big and over-confident, Stan Laurel is small and timid; Bud Abbott is a cranky straight-man, Lou Costello is a cherubic fool. Elwood and Veta are likewise great foils for one another. To Veta's credit, she finally realizes that she values her brother just the way he is, moments before he is about to receive an injection that will render him more 'normal.' The taxi driver, who has transported many a patient after a similar injection, is quick to point out that they come back from the sanatorium as regular people, "and we know what stinkers they can be!"

### TRICKY BIT:

A large part of Elwood's generosity and thoughtfulness consists of offering people a drink. He and Harvey favor martinis – pretty much at any hour of the day. That being said, we almost never see Elwood actually take a drink, much less appear visibly drunk. It seems that alcohol is more a medium of conviviality than a crutch or an addiction. The bar that Elwood favors is reminiscent of a European café or pub, in the sense that it is a warm and welcoming public space where people can spend unpressured time together. The consumption of alcohol seems entirely secondary to the creation of a social and communal space. In a sense, Elwood's trips to the bar also serve as a kind of red herring, allowing us the option of discounting Harvey's existence as an alcoholic hallucination. There is a rich harvest of teachable moments available here, from the appropriate use of alcohol to tolerance of eccentricity, to the question of what we value in people, to the reality of the unseen or the redeeming power of imagination…and more.

## APRIL

MUSICAL/ROMANCE

# Easter Parade

*1948, 107 minutes, color*

**Featuring Fred Astaire, Judy Garland, Peter Lawford, Ann Miller, Jules Munshin.** *Directed by Charles Walters, written by Sidney Sheldon, Frances Goodrich and Albert Hackett, songs by Irving Berlin*

If your spirits should ever need a lift, there is no better tonic than a Fred Astaire movie. The stories are usually fast-paced, romantic and funny – and the dancing is always exhilarating. Where Gene Kelly has virile athleticism, Fred Astaire is all elegance and class, and in his world troubles are as light as the air he seems to be dancing on. Our family has yet to meet an Astaire movie we *didn't* like, but for sheer non-stop smile potential you might as well start with *Easter Parade*. It is not one of the products of his famous pairing with Ginger Rogers. But it is in color, it features the exceptional talents of both Judy Garland and Ann Miller and, number for number, it delivers a huge bang for the buck. Like many of his musicals it tells a story about people who are in show business, a device that allows an organic justification in the story for one fabulous song and dance routine after another.

*Easter Parade* is not specifically for people who celebrate Easter. It is simply book-ended by the annual holiday parade down Fifth Avenue, for which New Yorkers turn out to promenade in their finest finery. And if Jewish songwriter Irving Berlin can have one of the characters sing "I could write a sonnet / About your Easter bonnet," anyone can certainly enjoy the extravagant chapeaus on display. The movie opens with Fred Astaire (as performer Don Hewes) on a shopping spree for his dancing and (he hopes) romantic partner, Nadine, played by Ann Miller of the fabulous legs. On entering a toy store he spots "a bunny for my honey," but has to contend with a tow-headed youngster who has claimed the stuffed rabbit for himself. This Astaire does by demonstrating to the boy how enjoyable toy soldiers can be – and how akin tap-dancing is to drumming. This number alone is spectacular fun, but it is just the beginning.

Nadine is willing to accept Don's tributes, but not his heart (in spite of a touching rendition of "It Only Happens When I Dance with You"). She has decided to break up the act and strike out on her own – and she seems to have a bit of a soft spot for a mutual friend, Johnny, played by Peter Lawford. So Don Hewes is suddenly single, in every sense, and in the market for a new dancing partner. In the club where he goes to drown his sorrows, he makes a rash vow that he can pick any girl out of a chorus line and bring her along until she outshines the haughty Nadine. And from the group of girls performing a number on stage he chooses, almost at random, Judy Garland. Good choice.

Except that he learns, at rehearsal the next morning, that young Hannah Brown from Michigan literally doesn't know her left leg from her right. Don persists, all the same, in his sort of Pygmalion project – with some delightfully clumsy dancing to show for his efforts. (Astaire and Garland both prove themselves to be terrific physical clowns in this film.) The project of turning Hannah into another Nadine finally founders and Don

*It features the exceptional talents of both Judy Garland and Ann Miller and, number for number, it delivers a huge bang for the buck.*

realizes that she has plenty of talent and spunk of her own. Try turning Judy Garland loose on the Berlin classic "I Love a Piano" and you'd reach the same conclusion. So the new dancing team of Hannah and Hewes is born – and takes off.

Meanwhile, Johnny (Peter Lawford) has met Hannah in a rainy doorway outside a soda shop, and fallen for her. Irving Berlin is among the most approachable of the great songwriters who have contributed to the Great American Songbook. Where Cole Porter dazzles with sophisticated and unexpected rhymes, Berlin's lyrics lift almost imperceptibly from the realm of everyday speech, and are often at their most charming when they sound like just the kind of thing a regular fellow would say to his girl. So Johnny buys an umbrella from a pushcart vendor and answers Hannah's inquiry as to who he is with "I'm just a fella, A fella with umbrella, Looking for a girl who saved her love for a rainy day..." Hard to resist. Peter Lawford, handsome and eternally eligible, married into the Kennedy family and was a member of Hollywood's Rat Pack. He is the kind of guy that any girl would naturally fall for – unless his competition happened to be Fred Astaire. (Lawford also shows up in *Royal Wedding*, the film where Astaire famously dances on the ceiling.)

This is a world in which people wear fabulous clothes and live in fabulous apartments or hotel rooms. They also frequent, and explore their romantic misunderstandings in, a fabulous restaurant. Jules Munshin, fresh out of vaudeville, has a delightful turn as the seen-it-all waiter who can't seem to get his guests to stay and enjoy a meal. He does succeed in pantomiming his specialty salad for Hannah and the Professor. The high-toned headwaiter as physical clown has never been done better (the French maitre d' who presides over the bungled marriage proposal in *Spiderman 3* almost certainly owes something to Mr. Munshin's performance).

We get more superb physical clowning with Astaire and Garland as a "Couple of Swells" with tongue-in-cheek aspirations. Astaire gets to do some loose-limbed, just plain fantastic dancing in "Steppin' Out with My Baby." Ann Miller, who danced well into her '60s, has several great numbers of her own as Nadine, most notably an exuberant rendition of "Shakin' the Blues Away."

**TRICKY BIT:**

Nadine has an African-American maid and Don has an Asian manservant. These characters do not transcend the stereotypes of the time in any way, but neither do they evoke more than a momentary wince.

## APRIL

### DRAMA/CRIME/THRILLER

# The Defiant Ones

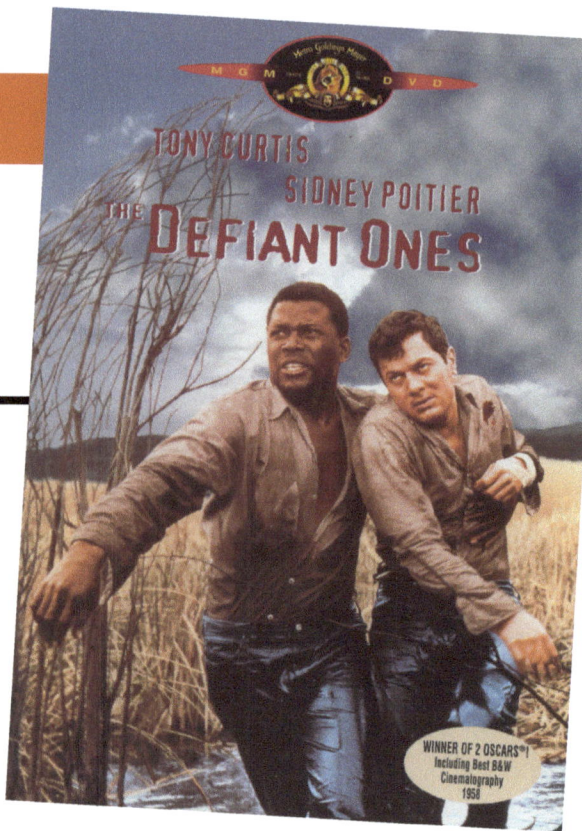

*1958, 97 minutes, black-and-white*

**Featuring Tony Curtis, Sidney Poitier, Theodore Bikel, Charles McGraw, Cara Williams, Lon Chaney.**
*Directed by Stanley Kramer, written by Harold Jacob Smith*

The 'Golden Age of Hollywood' was far from golden for non-white performers. Except in the instance of some all-black shows (like *Stormy Weather* or *Cabin in the Sky*), an actor of color or ethnicity could mainly expect to portray members of the serving class or mysterious and inscrutable foreigners. One man finally broke the color barrier in movies, as Jackie Robinson did in 1947 in major league baseball. Anyone who overcomes prejudice to open a door for opportunity (as Jackie Robinson did - and no doubt other examples come to mind) is likely to need more than ordinary courage, character and talent. Poise and a photogenic appearance don't hurt. All these characteristics can be found in the first black actor in Hollywood to establish himself as a leading man and a bona fide movie star: Sidney Poitier. Although there are still great challenges for actors of color, the performers who languished under the restriction of the old stereotypes would hardly have been able to imagine the range of career opportunities available to African-American, Asian-American and other performers who have walked through the door that Poitier opened for them.

Poitier's good looks, his great talent, his inner dignity and the intensity of his screen presence are all major contributors to his success. But perhaps one reason that he remains such an inspiring figure is that he achieved his success not by avoiding the conflicts inherent in being a black man in a white business, but by embracing them. His characters are often powered by rage at the racism they experience – and they express their feelings forcefully. A beautiful example is his character of Noah Cullen in *The Defiant Ones*. Directed by Stanley Kramer, this is a film that zooms in on the issue of race through a simple but powerful story device: a black convict and a white convict escape from a Southern prison chain gang...but despite the fact they hate each other, their fates are inextricably linked. They are literally shackled together.

The opening scene, in which the truck carrying the convicts overturns in a nighttime accident, is somewhat murky and hard to follow. However, it isn't long before dawn shows us a very clear picture indeed: the two convicts hunted through the countryside like animals, followed not only by a posse but by trained bloodhounds (who receive more tender consideration from their handler than their human quarry could ever hope for). The prisoners' situation is scary, and the animosity between them is painful. And yet it is a completely engaging pleasure to spend time with two of the handsomest, most charismatic leading men Hollywood ever produced: Poitier and Tony Curtis. They are both young and strong in this picture, and the sweat on their backs is real as they run and scramble through the backwoods.

As they narrowly escape death or capture, the two men's hostility and prejudice toward each other gradually develops into understanding, sympathy and genuine affection. They encounter a young boy near the farm he shares with his mother, and seize the chance for food and sanctuary. Finally the men are able to break their iron shackles, but their interdependence is now complete. Tony Curtis's "Joker" Jackson has to insist that the woman of the house feed Noah as well as himself. Abandoned by her husband, she is drawn to "Joker" and makes plans to run off with him. Only after Noah takes his leave does she

*The first black actor in Hollywood to establish himself as a leading man and a bona fide movie star: Sidney Poitier.*

admit to "Joker" that she has sent his compatriot off through the swamp, there to be swallowed up in quicksand. "Joker" is a changed man - he follows his friend, and helps Noah through the swamp to dry land. Noah is able to jump a passing train and holds out his hand to "Joker" to help him climb aboard. It's an incredible shot: the black hand and the white hand reaching out to one another, no longer physically shackled but now inextricably bound through friendship and loyalty. The suspense in the film is beautifully maintained throughout, so we won't ruin it here by revealing the ending.

Academy Award-nominated performances abound in this movie. Theodore Bikel (also known from his career as a folksinger) was nominated as Best Supporting Actor for his warm and sympathetic performance as the sheriff who hunts the two men reluctantly, only under threat of losing his own job. Lon Chaney, Jr. (who is recognizable from his famous role as the Wolf Man) plays an ex-convict who manages to prevent the two men from being lynched in a small town they get caught in. Cara Williams was also nominated as the abandoned wife, whose bigotry interacts with her own desperate self-interest in trying to pry Noah and "Joker" apart. Poitier and Curtis were both nominated for Best Actor. Although neither won for this picture, Curtis gets some credit for insisting that Poitier get top billing.

Perhaps the nicest irony in the film is that blue-eyed Tony Curtis, with a string of "pretty boy" roles behind him, should be cast as the ignorant white bigot. But then, his character's transformation might perhaps be informed by some personal experience. He was born Bernard Schwartz in the Bronx, but managed to pass for years as Gentile. (In this he had lots of company. Among the Jewish Hollywood stars who "passed": Kirk Douglas, Edward G. Robinson, Paul Newman, Tony Randall, among many others).

### TRICKY BITS:

In the early parts of the film, "Joker" calls Noah "nigger" and "boy." The filmmaking is skillful enough to show us that "Joker" is parroting words and attitudes he has absorbed from his environment, without reflection. His growing friendship with Noah provides both a reality check and a redemption for his character. On another subject, there is a suggestion that some intimacy occurs between "Joker" and the farm wife during the night. However, the implication is tastefully handled and is unlikely to raise questions, since the point being made is simply that the two are sufficiently attracted to each other to consider running away together.

# APRIL

# Animated Film Night

Treat yourselves to an evening of cartoons! Perhaps to some parents that doesn't sound like much of a treat. If you've seen nothing but cartoons for a number of years, and some of those over and over again, it can be hard to remember that some of these animated films are true classics. There is bound to be one you somehow never got around to seeing – or you're due to see again because you didn't pay attention, the first time around, to how beautifully made it was. Animated features have come in to their own recently, vying for Academy Awards on an equal footing with live-action films. But they were taken just as seriously by the early practitioners of the art.

Walt Disney elicits many a raised eyebrow from adults who are used to seeing the 'Disney version' of a story rendered saccharine and toothless. In his earliest years, however, Disney pursued a very high standard in each of his animated films, pouring the full resources of his studio and highly skilled artists into each film (eventually about one each year). Many of them contain scenes and characters which are plenty frightening for younger children, and can probably be more happily revisited when they are older. Disney was considered crazy when he started work on *Snow White and the Seven Dwarfs*, the first full-length Technicolor animated feature in English. Audiences were accustomed to cartoon 'shorts' before the feature at a matinee. When *Snow White* premiered in 1937 it immediately became a huge hit and the highest-grossing film in movie history until *Gone with the Wind* came along in 1939. It is credited with inspiring the makers of another full-length fantasy that came along soon after, *The Wizard of Oz*, and certainly created a new and much-loved film genre. Many animation techniques which were developed for the movie became standard in the industry. The songs are memorable, the characters are well delineated, the witch is truly scary and there are lots of delightful little gags sprinkled throughout. (Sid Caesar did a very funny episode in his '50s TV series, *Your Show of Shows*, in which he places a bet on being able to remember the names of all seven dwarfs.)

Disney's next animated feature, *Pinocchio* (1940), came along a few years later and also holds up well. It manages to retain some of the Old World feel of the original Collodi story about a puppet without strings who wants to be a real boy. Even the sweetness of the drawing style does not obscure some of the darker elements of the story: the shysters who waylay Pinocchio on the way to school, the puppetmaster who keeps him in a cage, or his exile to Pleasure Island where any form of destructive behavior goes. A young boy named Lampwick undergoes a spectacular and frightening transformation into a donkey. In another great episode, Pinocchio is reunited with his father Geppetto inside the belly of a whale. On the other hand, Geppetto's hand-carved creations are lovingly lingered over, Jiminy Cricket provides the voice of conscience (and friendship), and Pinocchio does learn through his journey of adventure to be brave and honest enough to become a real boy. Again, the music is memorable, particularly the song "When You Wish Upon a Star."

*Fantasia* (1940) is often cited as a must-see classic. In it, Disney pairs episodes of animated action with classical music conducted by Leopold Stokowski, the most famous segment being Mickey Mouse in 'The Sorcerer's Apprentice.' Some will find it an easier film to admire than love. It is certainly ambitious and technically accomplished, and all that good music makes it feel so – well, *good for you*. Some segments are scary, some lyrical, some comical – but the lack of a narrative throughline makes it easy to tune in and out.

Our hearts go out more to *Dumbo* (1941), which is considerably shorter (64 minutes to *Fantasia*'s 120). The little elephant who is ridiculed for his big ears, and then learns that they enable him to actually fly – what greater affirmation could there be for people who feel small and powerless (and we don't just mean the kids)? Dumbo is a non-verbal character, which fits comfortably into the

world of circus and clowns that he inhabits. His silence is more than compensated for by the talkative mouse friend who sticks up for him. Timothy, who winds up as Dumbo's manager, is an original and delightful creation – long before Disney films became over-populated with wisecracking animal sidekicks sporting New York dialects. The meltingly beautiful song "Baby Mine" comes at a low moment, when Dumbo's mother is imprisoned for defending him, and is followed by a scene in which Dumbo and Timothy inadvertently get drunk. The pink elephants on parade are a worthy rival to *Fantasia* and end with pink elephants tumbling through the air, morphing and changing into soft pink clouds in the (hung over) morning sky. One tricky bit here is the dark, shadowy figures of the roustabouts who pitch the Big Top in the opening of the show, and later a group of crows who are clearly African-American, and who sing a jazz-inflected number "When I See an Elephant Fly." Stereotypes, yes. And yet the crows are cool, smart, independent – and sympathetic to our sweet young hero. So with the right chat about cultural context, it is still possible to enjoy them for the sassy characters they are.

And then, of course, there is *Bambi* (1942). Lives there a child who has not had the opportunity to be traumatized by the death of Bambi's mother? This may be the ultimate "what do you mean you haven't seen" of animated films. What is striking about *Bambi* on rescreening it is the gentle, leisurely pace with which the story unfolds. It is a rare pleasure to be led into a world – in this case the beautifully drawn and detailed world of the forest – without a dramatic hook in the first ten minutes (now considered indispensable for pulling people into a movie), nothing violent or wrenching or startling. The special features that are part of recent DVD versions give a wonderful glimpse into the painstaking work of the artists who, long before computer-generated animation, created these hand-drawn feature-length movies cel by individual cel.

Leaving the world of Disney, there are extraordinary pleasures to be found in the compilations of Warner Brothers short animated films. Their Looney Tunes and Merrie Melodies series feature such classic tricksters as Bugs Bunny, Daffy Duck and Tweety-Bird (ever foiling the plans of Sylvester the cat). If you ever plan to show your kids *Who Framed Roger Rabbit*, they will get a bigger kick out of it if they are already familiar with the antics of Porky Pig, Elmer Fudd, Wile E. Coyote and Roadrunner, Yosemite Sam and the rest. The Merrie Melodies series was less focused on recurring characters, and more on single stories (sometimes classic tall tales or American legends). A frequent feature, though, is a great musical score (such as Disney used in his 'Silly Symphonies' series), which just goes to show that using classical music with cartoons was not an innovation in *Fantasia*.

Our family can always happily while away an evening or two with Betty Boop, thanks to a complete set of the Max Fleischer cartoons now available. Is Betty a kewpie-doll sex symbol or a feminist icon? The answer is yes. She may have always sported short skirts and a voice that reached to a high-pitched squeak ('boop-boop-be-doop – whee!"). But she also had her own car and her own house, and often a job, and was the first female character ever to anchor her very own cartoon series. Most importantly, her adventures are imaginative and often surreal. The black and white animation featured in her stories pulses with jazz music – literally. The characters sometimes simply bounce in rhythm, before the next fantastical occurrence. Popeye was another Max Fleischer creation, as was the Superman cartoon series. But Fleischer poured his wildest, most anarchic imagination into Betty…be sure to check her out.

# APRIL
### COMEDY/MUSICAL/ROMANCE

## Viva Las Vegas

*1964, 85 minutes, color*

**Featuring Elvis Presley, Ann-Margret, Cesare Danova, William Demarest, Nicky Blair.** *Directed by George Sidney, written by Sally Benson*

*Viva Las Vegas* is without doubt one of the towering pinnacles of American cinematic achievement. Well, not really. Not at all. But it is a great introduction to the one and only Elvis Presley. And if your children are not familiar with Elvis, how will they recognize his face in the window of the spaceship when it lands?

In all seriousness, Elvis Presley's impact on American popular culture was seismic. Many of his fans indeed found it impossible to accept his death, and generated a number of incredible theories as to how he must have cheated mortality. This was probably easier than embracing the astonishing array of overweight Elvis imitators in tight white suits – or the fact that Elvis himself, in his sad final years, seemed to have become a parody of this legion of wannabes. In his prime Elvis had talent, charm and charisma that were simply off the charts. They are all on display in *Viva Las Vegas*.

The movie is a high-spirited romp, full of beautiful young people singing and dancing and falling in love. In short: the sunniest, happiest form of American culture. Elvis had been making movies since *Love Me Tender*, his first outing in 1956. After a stint in the Army, he made more throughout the 1960s – there were 33 in all. For a while Elvis movies were a genre in themselves. Very few pleased the critics, but they were hugely successful with audiences and served as an engine to launch new hits for him, sparing him the need to make many live concert appearances. The formula usually involved Elvis in some vacation-oriented setting, surrounded by adoring girls (*Blue Hawaii* in 1961 aimed for some legitimacy by featuring Angela Lansbury as his mother, but remains primarily a musical postcard).

In *Viva Las Vegas* he is paired up with a girl who can more than hold her own with him: Ann-Margret, often referred to as the "female Elvis." Born Ann-Margret Olsson in Sweden, Ann-Margret grew up in the United States and was discovered by the comedian George Burns. Her career took off rapidly not only because she is a triple threat – singer, dancer, actress – but also because she is absolutely gorgeous. Their first number together, "The Lady Loves Me," is a sassy sing-off, balancing mutual attraction with plenty of attitude. It is not long before they are dancing together, Ann-Margret with every bit as much freedom and abandon as Elvis could give way to.

Elvis plays Lucky Jackson, a driver intent on winning the Las Vegas Grand Prix. Ann-Margret is Rusty Martin, the swimming instructor at a Vegas hotel. Lucky and Rusty's on-screen chemistry was reportedly fueled by an off-screen relationship between Elvis and Ann-Margret. (They stayed friends even once the romance cooled, and Elvis sent flowers to all of her opening night performances until he died in 1977.) Cesare Danova plays Count Elmo Mancini, Elvis's rival both for the car race and the girl. William Demarest plays Rusty's father – he was a member of Preston Sturges's stock company of actors (we see him as a Hollywood producer in *Sullivan's Travels*). But primarily the movie is a showcase for Ann-Margret, the shy young woman who turns into a bombshell on stage, and the King of Rock 'n' Roll, a working class boy who became an international sensation, by integrating black and white music in the 1950s, and then going on to sing it with all his soul.

## MAY

**CRIME/DRAMA/ROMANCE**

# On the Waterfront

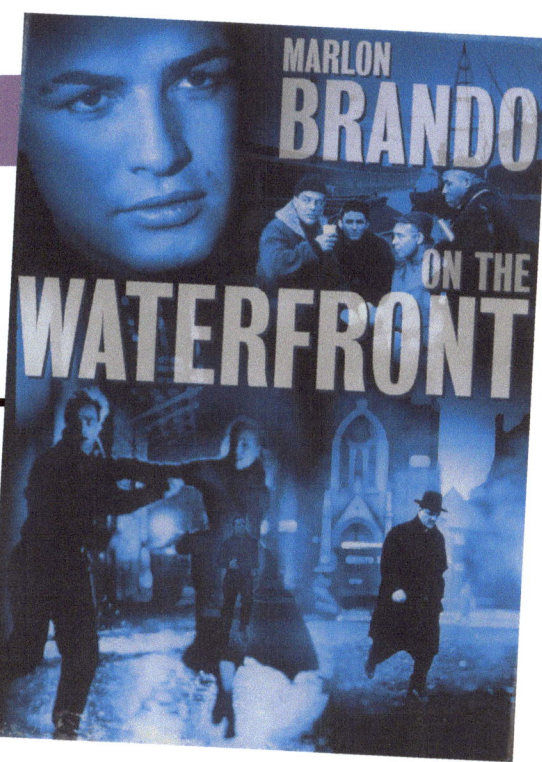

*1954, 108 minutes, black-and-white*

**Featuring Marlon Brando, Karl Malden, Lee J. Cobb, Rod Steiger, Eva Marie Saint.** *Directed by Elia Kazan, written by Budd Schulberg*

In many countries of the world May 1, or May Day, is not primarily associated with maypoles and the flowers that bloom in the spring. It is a celebration of the labor union movement and of workers' rights (like the right to an 8-hour work day, which was won in the U.S. after nationwide demonstrations on May 1, 1886). That makes it as good an occasion as any to watch *On the Waterfront*, a gritty movie at any time of year. This is not to say that the movie looks at labor unions through rose-colored glasses – far from it. The union depicted in this movie is *not* run according to the highest principles of the founders of the movement.

For all that it is a tough movie about a tough subject, our children followed the story with great interest and involvement. How do you handle bullies, when everyone is too frightened to stand up to them? Is it ever okay to tell on your friends? Is it sometimes the right thing to do, even though other people won't like you? What does it take to stand up for what's right? Stand up is literally what Marlon Brando's character has to do in order to win a moral victory over the corrupt union bosses who have a stranglehold on the waterfront. He can barely walk after the beating he gets from tough guy Johnny Friendly's thugs – but even so, he wins because he didn't back down from the fight.

The director in our family has a theory about great movies: until someone comes along who can do it better, a great movie just keeps improving with every year that passes. (Isn't that what defines a classic – that it just gets better with age?) It's also a way of saying, don't attempt a remake unless you think you can knock the original out of the ring. But who could ever knock *On the Waterfront* out of the ring? In it, the best and most exciting elements of the new American way of acting coalesced. The approach explored by the legendary Actors Studio in New York, in which acting became visceral, real and personal – the style which defines contemporary American acting – is exemplified here by an ensemble of players each at the peak of their game. We have a charismatic Marlon Brando in his prime, Eva Marie Saint in her luminous screen debut, and Karl Malden, Lee J. Cobb and Rod Steiger turning in memorable performances. We have Leonard Bernstein's only original movie score, a script meticulously researched and then written with perfect pitch by Budd Schulberg, and the unobtrusively masterful orchestration of it all by director Elia Kazan.

Brando's character, Terry Malloy, is a former boxer who has always put family loyalty ahead of personal ambition. His brother Charley (Rod Steiger) has become the lawyer for Johnny Friendly (Lee J. Cobb), a union boss who has been corrupted by ties to the mob. Friendly offers jobs unloading freighters at the docks, and protection, in exchange for kickbacks from the workers' pay and silence about his criminal connections. Terry's loyalty to his brother, and his brother's boss, has put him into two painful situations. In the first one, he was instructed to lose a fight that he was up for and ready to win – so that Johnny Friendly could make money on a bet. You'll probably recognize the lines with which Terry finally confronts his brother for not looking out for him: "I coulda been a contender. I coulda been somebody, instead of a bum which is what I am." Terry traded a shot at greatness as a prize-fighter for the life of a longshoreman, dependent on Friendly for jobs. The movie traces the way that Terry finally becomes somebody, even a hero, by not throwing a crucial fight.

The second painful situation is the one that opens the movie. We first meet Terry standing in the street and calling up to a window, urging a young man Joey Doyle to go up on the roof of his building to rescue one of the pigeons he keeps as pets. Shadowy figures are waiting on the roof, and before we know it the young man has fallen to his death. Terry has been given a bigger job than unloading cargo from ships – he has, without knowing it, set up the murder of a witness who was about to testify against Johnny Friendly. Terry thought they were just going to "lean on him a little" (as it turns out he too is going to get leaned on by the end of the story). Now, as the last man who was known to see Joey Doyle alive, he becomes a person of interest to the police pursuing the case.

One of the toughest challenges an actor can face is to play a character less intelligent than himself, without condescending to or flattening the character into cliché. Terry Malloy is a man of instinct and emotion, both of which Brando had in abundance. But Brando's (Academy Award-winning) achievement is to show, with respect and compassion, Terry's mental struggle to understand the dilemma he has been placed in, and how people can act the way they do. When it comes to action, he is led by loyalty and by his heart. So when he begins to fall in love with Joey Doyle's sister, Edie (Eva Marie Saint), Terry starts to wrestle with a new loyalty that comes with a new moral stance. His path toward doing the right thing is helped by Father Barry (Karl Malden), a bare-knuckle priest who learns that sometimes more than words are needed to fight the good fight. And sometimes the right words – like words spoken in court – are the only way to fight Johnny Friendly's code of "D and D" or deaf and dumb.

If Father Barry is the voice of Terry Malloy's conscience, Edie Doyle is his angel. A moment that happened spontaneously in one take famously wound up on screen: Edie drops her glove and Terry stoops to pick it up for her, then slips it on his own hand. It is a perfect image, unconsciously arrived at – he is trying on for size her way of viewing things, her way of being in the world. Terry also takes over looking after Joey Doyle's pigeons on the roof (it's just as well no one mentions the connection with the word "stoolpigeon"). Not only is Terry wracked with guilt for his part in Joey's death, but he has to see young kids growing up loyal to the code of D and D, which he himself has finally seen through. We know how much courage it takes for Terry to stand up in court and be a contender, partly because of the terrible fates that witnesses seem to meet. The visual power of the threat is reinforced by casting: at least three of Johnny Friendly's thugs are played by former professional fighters.

*The style which defines contemporary American acting is exemplified here by an ensemble of players each at the peak of their game.*

**TRICKY BITS:**

Terry's beating at the end of the film is meant to be brutal, but by today's standards it is not graphic in any unexpected way. One disturbing image is the discovery of the body of Terry's brother, killed to intimidate him into silence, and suspended on a hook in the alleyway. Again, the image is shocking for emotional reasons, but if your family has seen any recent superhero or action movies, you are likely to have seen as bad or, probably, much worse.

More tricky for adults, perhaps, is the question that dogged Elia Kazan through most of his career: that of his testimony before the House Un-American Activities Committee during the McCarthy era. Kazan appeared as a 'friendly' witness and, despite the mastery he may have displayed as a director, his reputation in the film world has been a divisive one ever since. When he was given a Lifetime Achievement Award by the Motion Picture Academy in 1999, many of his colleagues gave him a standing ovation – while others pointedly remained seated. Some look at *On the Waterfront* as Kazan's self-justifying argument in favor of ratting on your friends. Brando was already a star when *On the Waterfront* was being cast, largely because of his performance as Stanley in Tennessee Williams' *A Streetcar Named Desire* in 1951, also directed by Kazan. Between the two movies, however, came Kazan's testimony – and Brando initially refused to work with him again. In a canny move, the producers arranged to have Karl Malden direct a scene from the screenplay at the Actors Studio with a new up and comer: Paul Newman. Sure enough, Brando was not about to let a plum role go to competition like that, and he signed. The debate over Kazan's testimony continues after more than fifty years. The moral issues explored in *On the Waterfront* will be talked about still longer.

## MAY
### FANTASY/MUSICAL

# Mary Poppins

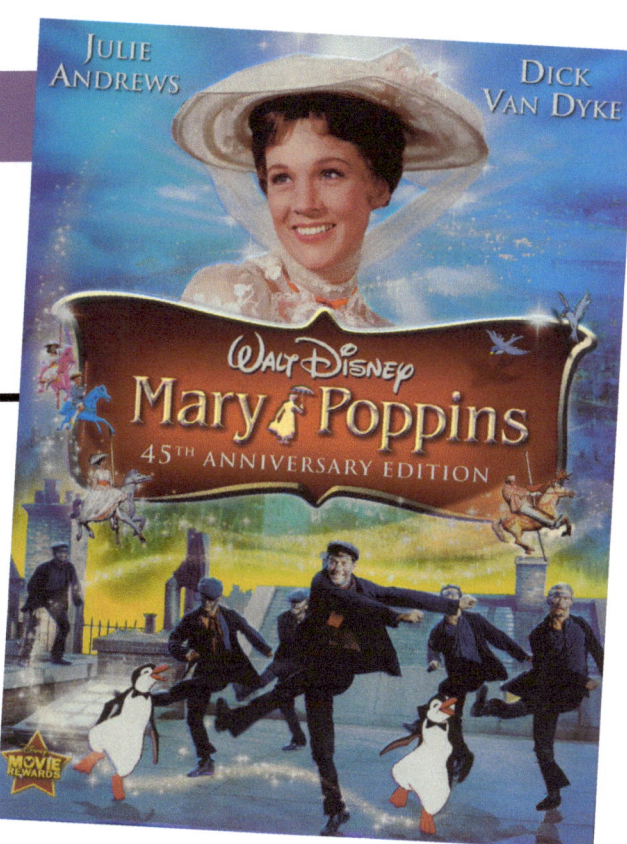

*1964, 139 minutes, color*

**Featuring Julie Andrews, Dick van Dyke, David Tomlinson, Glynis Johns, Hermione Baddeley, Elsa Lanchester, Arthur Treacher, Ed Wynn, Jane Darwell. Directed by Robert Stevenson, screenplay by Bill Walsh and Don Da Gradi, original music by Richard M. Sherman and Robert B. Sherman; based on the series of books by P.L. Travers**

If you ask a kid what they like best about *Mary Poppins*, they are likely to answer "the magic." If you ask an adult, they may not be able to answer so succinctly, but it is probably the chance to visit (for a while) a childhood that feels safe, secure and innocent – and full of magic. At the opening of the movie, Mary Poppins sits on a cloud, with her carpetbag slipping through it a couple of times in homage to the baby elephant about to be delivered by the stork in *Dumbo*. She hovers above the city of London: maybe a London that never really existed, but it certainly looks like an enchanting place to grow up.

The series of Mary Poppins books by P.L. Travers, on which the movie is based, are set in 1930s London. The film takes place instead in the Edwardian period, which feels like perhaps a somewhat warmer time - and easier to idealize. It was an age of optimism and confidence (as extolled by Mr. Banks in the song "The Life I Lead"). This is one of many changes that distressed Ms. Travers, who for a couple of decades denied Walt Disney the rights to the story and then, having finally given in, complained that the film version softened the character and the world she had created. (The stage version of *Mary Poppins*, which has since been revived, attempts to return some of the darkness and edge to the story.)

In the words of the famous song, "a spoonful of sugar helps the medicine go down." But it is a mistake to think there is anything saccharine in the lives of Jane and Michael Banks, the children in the film. They have a flighty, neglectful mother, an authoritarian and distant father, and are abandoned to the care of a series of dour, sour nannies. The latest, Katie Nana, is played by Elsa Lanchester (famous for her portrayal, in younger years, of the Bride of Frankenstein). When the Banks children's pursuit of childlike fun finally drives Katie Nana to quit, an ad in the Times summons a long line of prospective nannies outside the Banks family's door on Cherry Tree Lane. "Ghastly-looking crew!" is the assessment of their eccentric nautical neighbor, Admiral Boom – and indeed they are. (Many of the middle-aged, black-outfitted nannies were actually played by men in drag.) It is pure delight when the wind picks up and literally blows the nannies away...and Mary Poppins floats in from above with her umbrella serving as a parasail. Mary Poppins turns out to be the medicine the Banks family needs in order to heal.

The ordered world Mr. Banks (who is, aptly, a banker) so values is a world of hierarchy. The first bit of medicine Mary Poppins administers upon her arrival is turning that hierarchy upside down by interviewing Mr. Banks to see whether he will measure up as an employer. When he looks confused at this, she asks "Excuse me – are you ill?" The 'treatment' goes on. Mary not only ensures that the children enjoy some fantastical outings, like the extended animated sequence which features the song 'Supercalifragilisticexpialidocious,' but also that they consort with a bunch of chimney-sweeps – close to the bottom of the social ladder on which the Banks family occupies an upper rung. Through a wonderful intuitive stroke of casting (and apparently at the actor's suggestion), Dick Van Dyke plays not only Bert, the chimney-sweep and jack-of-all-trades, but also the senior Mr. Dawes, the

> **Mary Poppins** *made a screen star of young Julie Andrews and, with 5 Oscars wins out of 13 nominations, was a great feather in Walt Disney's cap.*

chairman of the bank: both the bottom and the top of the hierarchy.

Mary's mission is not so much about the children: her aim is to change the parents. Once Mr. Banks has gotten caught in her topsy-turvy orbit, his transformation is inevitable…from self-satisfied prig on top…to disgraced outcast on the bottom…to loving father, who is finally able to see the beauty and value of his children, just as they are. He mends the four pieces of their kite, like knitting together the four members of the family, and Mrs. Banks provides the tail by giving up her suffragette ribbon for the cause of a united family. The joyous anthem 'Let's go fly a kite' is a reminder of all the images in the film of rising above stuffy social confines: the birds the children want to feed with their tuppence, the tea-party on the ceiling in which laughter lifts people right off the ground, the buoyant chimney sweeps popping up onto the rooftops to dance, and even old Mr. Dawes himself, finally airborne because of the power of a joke.

*Mary Poppins* made a screen star of young Julie Andrews and, with 5 Oscar wins out of 13 nominations, was a great feather in Walt Disney's cap. (Julie Andrews hesitated at first to take the part, hoping to be cast in the film version of *My Fair Lady* in the role of Eliza Doolittle, which she had originated on Broadway. The part went to Audrey Hepburn instead – but Julie Andrews walked off with the Best Actress Oscar.) Robert Stevenson was nominated for Best Director, the first person to be nominated in that category for a Disney film. One of the film's wins on Oscar night was for Best Music Score, and indeed Richard M. Sherman and Robert B. Sherman made a huge contribution to the success of the picture. Sons of a Tin Pan Alley songwriter, their credits include wonderful songs for many Disney and other films (including *The Jungle Book, The Aristocats, Chitty Chitty Bang Bang, Winnie the Pooh* and *Charlotte's Web*).

Many of the performances in the movie are memorable for their charm. The dance number 'Step in Time' features some spectacularly athletic moves from the chorus of chimney-sweeps on the rooftops of London. Dick Van Dyke holds his own with that high-stepping crew, in spite of giving his character Bert what is (famously) one of the worst Cockney accents ever attempted by an American actor. Ed Wynn, the veteran vaudevillian, wisely opted not to attempt an accent at all – and reportedly the director gave him free rein to improvise as he bobbed about on the ceiling as Uncle Albert, cracking old chestnuts of jokes.

Other veterans on view include Arthur Treacher (who made a career as the quintessential English butler) playing the local bobby, and Jane Darwell of *The Grapes of Wrath* seen here, in her last screen performance, as the Bird Lady. David Tomlinson does a lovely job of tracing Mr. Banks's journey from pompousness to vulnerability (he went on to star in another children's classic, *Bedknobs and Broomsticks* with Angela Lansbury, and with music again by the Sherman Brothers). And Glynis Johns (remember her in *The Court Jester*?) is lovely as Mrs. Banks, indulgently propping up her husband's puffed-up ego at home, while marching for women's rights on the street.

The Sherman brothers, in one of their many contributions to the film, suggested that she become a suffragette in order to explain why she might be so preoccupied and neglectful of her children. The only unfortunate aspect of this choice, meant to soften and redeem her character, is that when she gives up her suffragette ribbon to make a tail for the childrens' kite, the story might seem to end on an anti-feminist note. Then again, the very final scene goes to Mary Poppins herself who, no matter how attached she gets to the children she cares for, must take flight again when the wind changes: always independent, and practically perfect in every way.

## MAY

**DRAMA/FAMILY**

# I Remember Mama

*1948, 134 minutes, black-and-white*

**Featuring Irene Dunne, Barbara Bel Geddes, Oskar Homolka, Philip Dorn, Sir Cedric Hardwicke, Edgar Bergen, Rudy Vallee.** *Directed by George Stevens, written by DeWitt Bodeen, based on a play by John Van Druten*

Mother's Day falls in May, and gives us an opportunity to celebrate all that is good and wonderful in motherhood and mothers. Who better to spend the holiday with than a mother who is beautiful, loving, self-sacrificing…and has a soft Norwegian accent? In other words, Irene Dunne in *I Remember Mama*. If Ms. Dunne's portrayal reminds you of your own mother, you are very fortunate. But even if your mother happens to rival Joan Crawford in *Mommie Dearest* mode, this film will offer you warm smiles and the odd tear with which to mark the holiday.

Not only does it offer a charming family story, *I Remember Mama* is set in San Francisco, that most photogenic of cities and George Stevens' hometown, in the 1910's (a few years after the great earthquake). The story is told through the memory of Katrin Hanson, the oldest daughter of the family, now grown up to be a writer. This character is based on Kathryn Forbes, on whose memoir ("Mama's Bank Account") the movie is based. The story also had an earlier incarnation on Broadway, the play by John Van Druten being produced by Rodgers and Hammerstein. A long-running television series in the 1950s, featuring Peggy Wood, was to follow – and then it made a brief appearance as a musical in 1979 (Richard Rodgers's last), starring Liv Ullmann and George Hearn.

The family are Norwegian immigrants, drawn to San Francisco by opportunity and the desire to stick together and maintain old values in the new world. These include self-reliance and thrift. As Mama goes through the week's expenses on Saturday night, and counts out a few coins for each from Papa's wages as a carpenter, she is happy to be able to conclude "Is good. We don't have to go to the bank." Another is keeping promises. When Dagmar, the youngest daughter, is admitted to hospital for an operation, Mama learns that the nursing staff won't allow her to keep her promise to be there when her daughter wakes up. This is so counter to her deeply held belief that children should feel secure, that Mama contrives to slip into the children's ward at night disguised as a member of the cleaning staff. She enters literally on her hands and knees, in time to comfort the newly awakened Dagmar and sing the entire ward of children to sleep.

Is this family too good to be true? Not at all. They are entirely human. There are a couple of battle-axe aunts, ready to laugh at shy Aunt Trina's plans to marry the undertaker Mr. Thorkelson – until they are threatened by Mama with the revelation of family secrets. And there is Uncle Chris, the head of the family, whose loud, gruff manner scares the children (and conceals his tender concern for them). Oskar Homolka, the only holdover from the Broadway cast, makes Uncle Chris entirely endearing. Yes, he drinks a little – and he scandalizes the battle-ax aunts by neglecting for years to tell them that he has actually married his housekeeper, whom they have only referred to as "the woman."

This is only one of the many fine performances by well-known actors. Rudy Vallee plays the doctor who oversees Dagmar's treatment. Edgar Bergen, who was famous for his ventriloquist act with Charlie McCarthy, and for being the father of Candice Bergen, plays the timid suitor to timid Aunt Trina ("Uncle Chris will eat him!" is

> *Every shot is beautifully staged by director George Stevens (who went on to make **Shane**, among other greats).*

the assessment of one of the aunts). Ellen Corby is a tremulous Aunt Trina – we last saw her as Humphrey Bogart's secretary in *Sabrina*. Sir Cedric Hardwicke plays the down-on-his-luck boarder who reads to the family every evening from the great works of literature – and leaves behind his library as payment for his room. Barbara Bel Geddes, who later became a mainstay of the TV series *Dallas*, is here at the beginning of her career as Katrin Hanson. Peeking out from under Mama's earthy goodness is some of the sparkle that enlivened Irene Dunne's screwball comedies with Cary Grant. And every shot is beautifully staged by director George Stevens (who went on to make *Shane*, among other greats). This is one of those movies that looks for a moment as though it is going to be "good for you"...and then winds up delivering so many pleasures that it feels, instead, like a guilty treat.

# MAY

### ACTION/ADVENTURE/WAR

## The Guns of Navarone

*1961, 158 minutes, color*

**Featuring Gregory Peck, David Niven, Anthony Quinn, Anthony Quayle, James Darren, Stanley Baker, Irene Papas, Richard Harris.** *Directed by J. Lee Thompson, written by Carl Foreman, based on a novel by Alistair MacLean*

The Memorial Day weekend is often about picnics and barbeque, but it is also an opportunity to remember the bravery of men and women who have given their lives in times of war. War movies can be a hard genre to love for families. But *The Guns of Navarone* is an excellent choice for exploring the dilemmas and moral choices presented by armed conflict. Although it takes place in wartime, it is first and foremost a cracking good adventure story. It's not so much focused on combat or violence as it is on character. What's more, it is not set in some grim and gritty "war is hell" trench but, in keeping with the first unofficial weekend of summer, in the sun-soaked isles of Greece.

We had a tough time convincing our 8-year-old daughter to watch the movie, based on the title: she thought it was all about guns in some city somewhere. The guns referred to in the title are actually only two – two very big guns in a cliffside underground bunker on the island of Navarone. The gun emplacement menaces a key shipping channel through which the Royal British navy is due to sail in a few days, to relieve soldiers besieged on another island. The near-impossible mission faced by our team is to destroy the guns before they can inflict damage on the ships engaged in the rescue mission. *The Guns of Navarone* is a close cousin of caper or heist movies, in which a team is assembled for a job based on their disparate talents – usually for getting into secure locations and blowing things up. Think *Ocean's Eleven, Asphalt Jungle, Rififi, The Dirty Dozen*, and The Professionals (or the television shows which capitalized on the genre: *Mission: Impossible* and *It Takes a Thief*).

Gregory Peck plays Captain Keith Mallory, the experienced climber who is needed to get the team up the one cliff on the island that is so steep it is believed to be unguarded. Mallory winds up taking over as leader when the British army man in charge (Anthony Quayle as Major Franklin) is injured in the climb. David Niven plays the chemistry professor who is brought along for his skill with explosives: unflappable until he realizes that his supplies are being sabotaged. This Allied force is truly international. It also includes Anthony Quinn as Stavros, a colonel in the Greek army, which has been defeated by the occupying Nazi force. He bears a storm cloud on his brow, and a grudge toward Mallory in his heart, because of a personal tragedy that occurred during the invasion. Teen idol James Darren plays a Greek-American, Spyros, whose sister (played by noted Greek actress Irene Papas) is working with the partisans on Navarone. (Irish actor Richard Harris, who was known to one generation as King Arthur in *Camelot* and to a more recent generation as the first Dumbledore in the Harry Potter series, has a tiny part in an early scene. Watch for him as the gunnery sergeant in the mission briefing: the one with the completely unconvincing "Australian" accent.)

Somehow the team encounters Nazi forces at every turn, and it becomes evident there is a traitor in their midst. This adds a layer of suspense to an already dangerous mission, but also results in a stark lesson about how traitors are handled in times of war. There is a high-stakes experiment in whether deliberately planted disinformation can defeat a powerful truth serum called scopolamine. Perhaps most importantly, there is the

***The Guns of Navarone*** *is a close cousin of caper or heist movies, in which a team is assembled for a job based on their disparate talents.*

moral dilemma voiced by Captain Mallory. Gregory Peck has the square-jawed strength and quiet moral presence that brings special resonance to the conflict over whether the only way to win a war is to become as nasty as the enemy. Here is a man who becomes a hero not because he wants to be, but because he is essentially decent and knows that someone has to step up to the plate. (One can see why Peck made such an indelible imprint on the role of Atticus Finch in *To Kill a Mockingbird* the year after this film was released, winning him the Oscar for Best Actor.)

### TRICKY BIT:

If your family is extremely particular about salty language around kids, you may not enjoy the way the word 'bloody' gets tossed around in an early scene (as in, the mission is 'bloody' impossible). These are British soldiers in the Second World War – so it would be improbable for them not to speak that way. Kind of quaint now, with what we've become used to. In fact, your kids might be surprised to learn that the word was once considered off limits in polite society, and still isn't suitable in front of the grandparents. It may have originally been used to replace "By our Lady," which was considered sacrilegious for taking the name of the Virgin Mary in vain.

## MAY

### CRIME/MYSTERY/COURTROOM

# Witness for the Prosecution

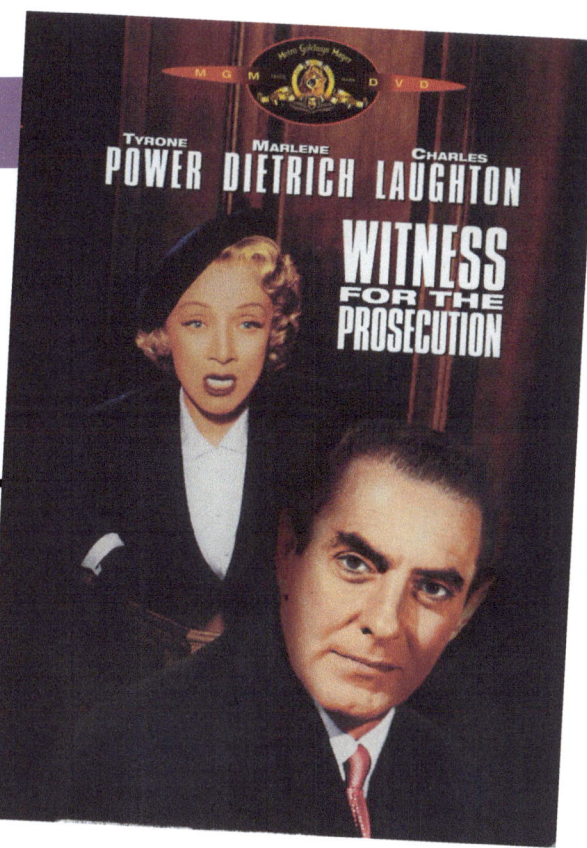

*1957, 116 minutes, black-and-white*

**Featuring Tyrone Power, Marlene Dietrich, Charles Laughton, Elsa Lanchester, John Williams, Norma Varden, Una O'Connor.** *Directed by Billy Wilder, screenplay by Larry Marcus, Billy Wilder and Harry Kurnitz, based on the story and play by Agatha Christie*

"The management of this theatre suggests that for the greater entertainment of your friends who have not yet seen the picture, you will not divulge the secret of the ending of *Witness for the Prosecution*." So says the voice of a reasonable-sounding man as the closing credits roll, and we will honor that request. It is indeed an exceptional twist, coming at the end of a suspenseful tale. Dame Agatha Christie excelled at this kind of thing, which may explain why her mysteries have attracted more readers in the world than any other writing except for Shakespeare and the Bible. *Witness for the Prosecution* started as a short story and then was adapted by Ms. Christie, with her natural flair for drama, for a successful life on the stage. (Her play *The Mousetrap* has run continuously on the London stage since its opening in 1952, shattering all records for the length of an initial theatrical run.) To Ms. Christie's masterful hand with a thriller, the movie adds several major stars and director/screenwriter Billy Wilder's signature mordant wit (which we have encountered in *Sabrina* and *Some Like It Hot*).

Leonard Vole, accused of murder, is played by the handsome and charming Tyrone Power. A swashbuckling hero in the '30s (with movies like *The Mark of Zorro*), Power's name was synonymous in Hollywood with sex appeal and star power. He was the third generation of an acting dynasty (his children now making the fourth). Power had tried to escape his heroic image by playing a con man in *Nightmare Alley* in 1947 and, disillusioned with his career, was looking for more serious parts around the time that Wilder cast him in *Witness for the Prosecution*. He does a fine job of walking the line with Vole, making him utterly winning and yet apparently one of life's losers. Sadly, it was to be his last complete film. In the middle of shooting a dueling scene in his next movie, Power died of a massive heart attack at the age of 44, leaving his wife pregnant with his son Tyrone Power, Jr. Power is less recognizable to audiences today than some of his contemporaries, because his leading man years were cut short and he never had the opportunity to move into deeper, more complex roles.

Vole and his wife Christine make an exceptionally attractive couple. Christine is played by Marlene Dietrich, the German screen siren famous for her smoky singing voice and gorgeous legs. Dietrich was an overnight sensation in 1930 in *The Blue Angel* in her native Germany. She accompanied the director, Josef von Sternberg, to pursue her career in Hollywood, and established herself as a femme fatale throughout the '30s. Like Power, in many ways, she is better remembered than her movies are, and by the time she made *Witness for the Prosecution* she was still famous for being famous. It is a brilliant stroke of casting, and the script plays upon the English characters' distrust of Germans (especially so soon after World War II). Christine seems too cold, too disciplined, too in control to be trusted. When she appears as a witness for the prosecution, testifying against her husband, her treachery is shocking but – after all, what do we expect from a foreigner. Ahh, but the story is not over yet. Nor was Dietrich's own story. She did direct her career with

*In spite of its history in print and on stage, audiences had succeeded in keeping the secret of the ending so well that apparently the cast did not know it until they were ready to shoot the final scene.*

exceptional control and cool, continuing to sing her signature "Lili Marleen" to concert audiences until she was in her '70s. She had been a vocal opponent of the Nazi regime and spent much of the Second World War entertaining and heartening the Allied troops in the fight against her own country. Dietrich's personal style included trousers, which enhanced her noted bisexual appeal. A flashback scene in Witness for the Prosecution, in which we learn how Leonard and Christine met, lavished 145 extras, 38 stunt men and $90,000 on the opportunity to tear one of those pant legs off and reveal one of Dietrich's famous legs.

Agatha Christie's thriller unfolds in the courtroom and lawyer's chambers. The movie actually recreates a courtroom at the Old Bailey in London, so fans of courtroom drama get the added, somewhat exotic, treat of witnessing the pomp and powdered wigs of the English court. Billy Wilder's approach opens the story up and gives more focus to the character of the eccentric and brilliant barrister Sir Wilfred Robart. Recovering from a serious heart attack, Sir Wilfred is everywhere accompanied by a private nurse, Miss Plimsoll (a character created for the film). If she torments him by confiscating his cigars and fussing about naptime, he more than gets his own back with some verbal barbs. The impression that they are bickering like an old married couple plays somewhat on the fact that the actors, Charles Laughton and Elsa Lanchester, were actually married off-screen. Laughton, one of the first English actors to embrace film opportunities as well as theater, had a long and distinguished career. Like his co-stars, he scored great career triumphs in the 1930s, as a character actor rather than a leading man (Quasimodo in The Hunchback of Notre Dame and Captain Bligh in Mutiny on the Bounty are examples of his exceptional range). Elsa Lanchester was famous in her own right, having played the Bride of Frankenstein. Coming from an unconventional family, Lanchester's heart was always in vaudeville and music hall. Perhaps that is why she is able to be a good sport, and play such an effective comic foil for her husband, as he performs intimidating tricks with his monocle and nips brandy from a thermos in the courtroom. Her long devotion to a man of great talent is also reflected in her performance here. A couple of years into their marriage, Lanchester learned that Laughton was homosexual. She decided not to have children with him, which was a heartbreak for Laughton, who very much wanted to be a father. But she stayed with him, and they remained married for over three decades, until his death.

Alfred Hitchcock, the master of suspense, remarked that people often congratulated him on Witness for the Prosecution. With its riveting tension, plot surprises and droll character details, one can easily see why people would assume it was a Hitchcock film. Tell that to the Academy, who nominated Wilder for Best Director for the movie (Laughton and Lanchester were also nominated, as Best Actor and Best Supporting Actress). In spite of its history in print and on stage, audiences had succeeded in keeping the secret of the ending so well that apparently the cast did not know it until they were ready to shoot the final scene. We know that you will do your part too… enjoy the story, but mum's the word!

## JUNE
### COMEDY/MUSICAL/ROMANCE

# High Society

*1956, 111 minutes, color*

**Featuring Bing Crosby, Grace Kelly, Frank Sinatra, Celeste Holm, John Lund, Louis Calhern, Louis Armstrong.** *Directed by Charles Walters, screenplay by John Patrick, based on the play by Philip Barry, songs by Cole Porter*

Yes, we know. *The Philadelphia Story*, on which the musical *High Society* is based, is one of the all-time great film comedies. It is so good, in fact, with its breakneck pace and its rich social commentary, that it can be challenging to watch with younger children. When we first tried it, our 8-year-old asked about 15 questions during the first 10 minutes. By the time we got to the end of the movie (at almost 2 hours), she was a fan – but it was by no means certain that we would get through all of it. If your children are ready, by all means show them the black and white original, written expressly for Katharine Hepburn, and featuring a dryly sophisticated performance from Cary Grant and an Oscar-winning turn from James Stewart.

If you are not sure yet how you will fare with the original, we heartily recommend this musical adaptation. The story is all here, but introduced at a somewhat more leisurely pace (partly because of the presence of the songs). Grace Kelly plays the wealthy Tracy Lord, a young woman who is a little too good to be true, and finds herself finally wanting to come down off her pedestal. This was Kelly's last film role before she became Princess Grace of Monaco and, while she may lack Katharine Hepburn's razor-sharp intelligence and character, she certainly has the aristocratic demeanor and the perfection of her own blonde beauty.

One of the great bonuses of showing this film is that you get to introduce your family to several of the most important popular music figures of the 20th century. Bing Crosby, the great crooner, plays C.K. Dexter-Haven, Tracy's former husband who still loves her (the Cary Grant role). He is a supporter of the Newport Jazz Festival, which gives a justification for bringing music into the rarefied circles the wealthy Lord family move in. The film opens with a musical prologue by none other than the great Louis Armstrong, arriving on a bus with his band to play at the festival. Armstrong and his trumpet are featured in several more numbers. And the young reporter who is assigned to violate the privacy of Tracy's second wedding, and who almost steals her heart, is none other than old Blue Eyes himself, the legendary Frank Sinatra. The terrific comedy and social comment from Philip Barry are beautifully enhanced by the music of Cole Porter. Porter is the perfect songwriter for this world: witty, urbane and yet willing to touch the heart at just the right moment. His simple but perfect ballad, "True Love," became a hit single, and actually went platinum for Crosby and Kelly. Where Irving Berlin gives voice to regular guys and gals, Porter is the man for the sophisticated and heartbroken rich.

Apparently Tracy Lord ditched her first husband because he wrote a love song, using her middle name (the tender "I Love You, Samantha"). Writing the song might have been a lovely tribute, but allowing it to be played in public – how vulgar! Fortunately, Crosby can't help singing whenever he feels so moved. Nor can Sinatra, who sings the wonderful "You're Sensational" to Tracy's melting ice queen ("I don't care / If you are called the fair Miss Frigidaire / 'Cause you're sensational!") One of the best songs is saved for the encounter between Crosby and Sinatra. The producers realized the two musical giants didn't have a song together, and dropped in some vintage

*One of the great bonuses of showing this film is that you get to introduce your family to several of the most important popular music figures of the 20th century.*

Cole Porter for them, "What a Swell Party This Is!"

Tracy's would-be groom, played by John Lund, is easily out-classed by the men who surround her with music. What he offers is respectability, discretion, and a permanent place on the pedestal – in exchange for a responsible position in her father's firm. (The social climber groom is skewered somewhat more sharply in *Philadelphia Story*, but even here we can tell that, while Tracy may think she wants him, he is definitely not what she needs.) Tracy's jaundiced view of men may have its genesis in her philandering father. But Louis Calhern (who played both villain and fool in *Duck Soup*, as the nefarious leader of Sylvania) here becomes a figure of grace and dignity. He offers Tracy a lesson in accepting one's own humanity, and in the value of a wise and understanding spouse. Celeste Holm is wry and wise also, as the photographer who accompanies Sinatra on the mission to expose the Lord wedding to public view. She catches Uncle Willy's eye, but gamely fends him off, while waiting for her fellow reporter (Frank Sinatra's) wandering eye to find her again.

## JUNE

### COMEDY/ROMANCE

# Adam's Rib

*1949, 101 minutes, black-and-white*

**Featuring Spencer Tracy, Katharine Hepburn, Judy Holliday, Tom Ewell, David Wayne, Jean Hagen.**
*Directed by George Cukor, screenplay by Ruth Gordon and Garson Kanin*

# Pat and Mike COMEDY/ROMANCE/SPORTS

*1952, 95 minutes, black-and-white*

**Featuring Spencer Tracy, Katharine Hepburn, Aldo Ray, William Ching, Sammy White, George Mathews.**
*Directed by George Cukor, screenplay by Ruth Gordon and Garson Kanin*

Katharine Hepburn and Spencer Tracy were each movie stars in their own right. But their chemistry together, both on screen and off, was an important part of their respective legends. Contrast is essential for comedy, and it is also said in love that opposites attract. Hepburn was sharp, patrician and intelligent; Tracy had a gruff, macho, salt of the earth appeal. In one movie after another they fought the archetypal battle of the sexes. Off screen, their romance endured for decades. (Another iconic screen couple, Humphrey Bogart and Lauren Bacall, were able to marry and have children together. Tracy, who was Catholic, never felt free to divorce his wife, although he and Hepburn were discreet but devoted partners until his death.)

*Adam's Rib* is one of their most famous on-screen pairings, and is a delightful must-see (particularly for anyone who thinks that feminism was a new idea in the 1960s). Even more accessible for younger audiences, though, may be *Pat and Mike*, Hepburn and Tracy's next outing together.

In *Adam's Rib* they play a pair of lawyers, happily married to one another, who take on opposite sides of a case. Adam Bonner is assigned to prosecute a woman accused of shooting her errant husband (although she succeeds in doing little more than scaring him). Amanda Bonner, to her husband's dismay, decides to defend her. The farcical duel at the heart of the court case takes place between two brilliant practitioners of the "dumb blonde" stereotype: Judy Holliday and Jean Hagen. These ladies both appeared in the Broadway hit *Born Yesterday* and both were considered for the role of Lina Lamont in *Singin' in the Rain*. Here we get to enjoy both of them, although what they can see in the feckless husband played by Tom Ewell is anyone's guess.

They also provide a marvelous contrast with Katharine Hepburn's smart-as-a-whip Amanda. David Wayne has a scene-stealing turn as the neighbor across the hall who romances Amanda, unapologetically and in her husband's presence, with a love song he has written just for her (actually penned by Cole Porter). Yet this doesn't seem to damage the Bonners' marital bliss at all. They give charming dinner parties after a long day in court, call each

> *It is great fun to watch Katharine Hepburn, who was in reality a superb athlete, crumble on the golf green or in the middle of a tennis match.*

other Pinky, give each other His and Hers massages. It is only when Amanda sets out, in the courtroom, to prove the power of women that her happily egalitarian marriage shows signs of strain. Adam claims it is because she picked the wrong case, and is flouting the law by trying to win acquittal for a woman who is actually guilty as charged. We doubt him, though, and imagine his reactions really to be those of a threatened chauvinist – until he turns the tables on Amanda in surprising ways.

The merry battle of the Bonners proved so popular that the screenwriting team of Ruth Gordon and Garson Kanin were reunited with director George Cukor three years later for a rematch. *Pat and Mike* pairs Hepburn and Tracy as an unlikely couple – not married this time but still, in an odd way, meant for each other. Hepburn plays Pat Pemberton, a gifted golfer (and all-around athlete) who can't hit the broad side of a barn when her fiancé happens to be around. It is this premise which makes the story one that children can immediately relate to. Who, indeed, has not experienced that 'jinx' feeling when some certain someone is watching us try to accomplish a task? Whether that person is a tad critical, a little too nervous, or just someone we fervently want to impress – somehow their presence makes us fumble the ball, burn the sauce, and trip over our shoelaces or our tongues.

It is great fun to watch Katharine Hepburn, who was in reality a superb athlete, crumble on the golf green or in the middle of a tennis match. Her exceptional ability brings her to the attention of Mike Conover, a rather shady fight promoter (played by Tracy) who decides to become her manager. Pat does not quite understand the questionable figures who seem to surround Mike, and who want to own "a piece of her." But Mike believes in her as her fiancé does not, and she is game to go along with the partnership and find out what she is capable of achieving. Along the way we meet Aldo Ray, playing a fighter who feels jilted by Mike's passionate interest in his new client. The movie also features a number of professional athletes, famous in their time, in cameo roles. Few of them are familiar to us now, but if the film were remade today, it would be as if Tiger Woods or Venus and Serena Williams were invited to knock a few balls around with the star.

Hepburn and Tracy brought their shared sparkle of comedy and romance to a number of films: *Woman of the Year, State of the Union, Desk Set* and then the final movie of Tracy's career, *Guess Who's Coming to Dinner* (1967). This last pairing focuses on them as parents, struggling to accept Sidney Poitier as the young man their daughter brings home as a potential fiancé. The film was considered very liberal at the time, when intermarriage was uncomfortable for many and still illegal in a number of states. It has been pointed out that Poitier's character had to be a man of extraordinary accomplishment (not to mention the movie star good looks) in order to allow the white parents' to develop some degree of openness to him – and that perhaps those are the standards that still need to be met for people of ethnicity to move freely in an interracial setting. Whether that is still true or not, it was certainly true at the time, and Hepburn and Tracy made use of their star power to support a film that, although not critically acclaimed for its filmmaking, was certainly socially important in its time. Spencer Tracy died shortly after the movie was completed.

## JUNE
### COMEDY

# Life with Father

*1947, 118 minutes, color*

**Featuring William Powell, Irene Dunne, Elizabeth Taylor, Edmund Gwenn, Zasu Pitts, Jimmy Lydon.** *Directed by Michael Curtiz, written by Donald Ogden Stewart, based on a play by Howard Lindsay and Russel Crouse*

Dads deserve their own movie too, for Father's Day. *Life with Father* makes a nice companion piece with *I Remember Mama* because both are based on memoirs followed by highly successful stage plays and eventually television series. And here is the lovely Irene Dunne again, playing the patient and loving mother to a family in an old and more innocent time. There, however, the resemblance between the two films largely ends (although they appeared within a year of one another). The black and white photography in *I Remember Mama* enhances the sense of nostalgia for a time of sacrifice and family unity. The Technicolor world of *Life with Father* shows off the red hair sported by the four sons of the Day family and keeps us on the sunny, comic side of its patriarch's temper.

William Powell was nominated for the Best Actor Oscar for his characterization of banker Clarence ("Clare") Day: impossible, cantankerous and entirely lovable in spite of it. The setting is New York in the 1890's and we soon learn that Mr. Day likes things just so. We also see why everyone is anxious to accommodate him - as the smallest alteration in his preferred daily routine, such as the unauthorized intrusion of a new rubber plant in the drawing room, provokes an explosive "Oh, gad!" His first entrance in the film is built up with some suspense: the flurry of getting the breakfast table ready, then the sight of his shadow on the landing, then a pair of feet descending the stairs…and at least we see the tyrant himself. The new maid flees the house in sheer terror after walking into the study as Clare is ranting at a local politician. Since there is no one else in the room, she assumes that she is being addressed when Day booms, "You scalawag, we'll have you arrested!" And yet, a new dog introduced at the breakfast table is greeted with an indulgent smile. The news that one of the boys is pitching at his game that day is given a higher priority than learning his catechism. The man is a paper tiger. We learn to love him because of the skill with which William Powell (so cool and unflappable as Nick Charles in the *Thin Man* series) shows the tender heart within the gruff and combustible paterfamilias.

One can't help thinking again of Mr. Banks, the banker in *Mary Poppins*, declaring "It's the age of men!" It certainly is in this world, and we may have rather mixed feelings about it. In particular we may feel uncomfortable about Irene Dunne, so strong and stoic in *I Remember Mama*, here resorting to all the techniques women of the time used to "handle" their man: acting quizzical and confused about the household accounts, neglecting to tell him anything it might be inconvenient for him to hear, all the way up to crying and taking to her bed when the stakes get higher. Think of it as a sociological study of relations between the sexes in those days – and take a close look at who actually has the upper hand, when all is said and done. The issue on which Vinnie (Dunne) is finally willing to take a direct stand is whether or not her "Clare" will be baptized. You will see who wins.

One of the pleasures of the film is seeing a very young Elizabeth Taylor as the houseguest who romances the oldest son, Clarence Jr. Again, not everyone will relate to the great barrier that stands between the young couple: his family is Episcopalian and hers is Methodist. But we can all enjoy Edmund Gwenn as the minister whose grasp of

> *One of the pleasures of the film is seeing a very young Elizabeth Taylor as the houseguest who romances the oldest son, Clarence Jr.*

finances makes Vinnie look like a Wall Street whiz.

It may be difficult to find a good print of this movie. We watched one with poor sound quality, but the fun of the film was still well worth it with the sound cranked up. If the combination of print quality and the pre-feminist anthropology of the story are too much for you (or you don't want to give the father in your life too many ideas), consider the original *Cheaper by the Dozen* as an alternative.

Many people are familiar with the Steve Martin remake of *Cheaper by the Dozen* in 2003. The original (made in Technicolor, 1950, 85 minutes) is again based on a family memoir, and is certainly a very likable film. The relationship between Frank Gilbreth (played by Clifton Webb) and his wife Lillian (Myrna Loy) is more equitable than the marriage pictured in *Life with Father*. He is an efficiency expert, and she not only works alongside him but eventually takes over his business. Again, the eccentric father is the center of the story, but his passion for efficiency is a benign one, and does not yield the humor or depth of character we find in William Powell's portrayal of Clarence Day. The tone is droll rather than hilarious, and upon occasion more sentimental and even tragic. The chief novelty of the story lies in the dozen children the couple have set out to have and raise, six girls and six boys. (A visit from an advocate of birth control offers a classic moment of social awkwardness.) The oldest daughter, played by Jeanne Crain, is struggling to establish her independence as a young woman – but it turns out, of course, that her protective father is exactly the kind of parent all her peers dream of having. A sequel was made two years later, *Belles on Their Toes*, based on the next segment of the family memoir, about the mother and children after the father's passing.

Another portrait of a loving patriarch, who is out of step with the changing role his family needs him to play, can be found in *Meet Me in St. Louis* (1944). The setting is the first decade of the 1900s, when "Guess what – I've decided to move the family to New York" is just not going to cut it any more. And if you want to spend some more time with Spencer Tracy, watch him struggle in *Father of the Bride* (1950) to accept that his daughter (played by Elizabeth Taylor) is all grown up, ready to marry and fly the coop.

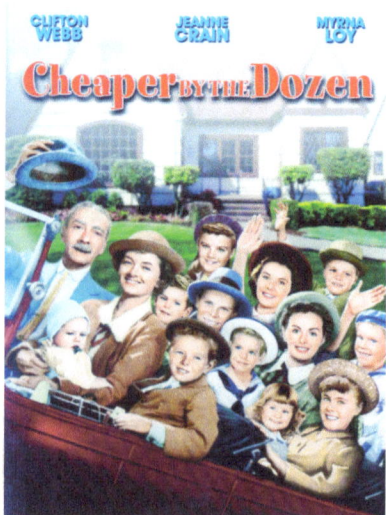

## JUNE
### ACTION/THRILLER/ADVENTURE

# Dr. No

*1962, 110 minutes, color*

**Featuring Sean Connery, Ursula Andress, Joseph Wiseman, Jack Lord, Bernard Lee, Lois Maxwell.** *Directed by Terence Young, screenplay by Richard Maibaum, Johanna Harwood, Berkeley Mather, based on a novel by Ian Fleming*

The name is Bond. James Bond. Ian Fleming's iconic British gentleman spy, 007 has endured through one incarnation after another, because we just can't seem to get enough of his adventures. *Dr. No* is the first Bond movie in a series which continues to thrive today, after 40 years and over 20 films. Sean Connery remains, for many, the quintessential James Bond. He made seven Bond films, and has been followed by estimable actors like George Lazenby, Roger Moore, Timothy Dalton, Pierce Brosnan and Daniel Craig. But Connery's imprint on the role is indelible. There are various stories about how he landed the role, who thought what about him, and how little success the studio originally expected from the first film. How the character and the series became so extraordinarily successful is easy to understand when you watch Sean Connery stalk through a shot with cool, feline grace (we are talking about one of the large, dangerous members of the cat family – not the house kitty variety). He is an athlete at the top of his game - fit, alert and level-headed – and we are always glad that he is playing for our team and not for the bad guys.

The first three in the series are classics (*Dr. No*, 1962, *From Russia with Love*, 1963, *Goldfinger*, 1964). The violence is fairly tame by contemporary standards, and the sexy interludes are tastefully suggested without anything explicitly shown. Lots of people smoke, and look cool doing it, and Mr. Bond is always ready for a vodka martini, shaken not stirred. Consider these teachable moments. Not only are these movies enjoyable for sheer escapist fantasy, they are the source for many of our favorite images of spies and adventure. There is always an element of straight-faced self-parody in the Bond films, which has given license to the creators of *In Like Flint, I Spy, The Man from U.N.C.L.E., Get Smart,* even the Indiana Jones series and, needless to say, Austin Powers and Johnny English.

*Dr. No* introduces many of the elements that have become a familiar part of the Bond world: the opening title sequence, the catchy theme music, Bond's cool demeanor at a gambling table, his ongoing flirtation with Miss Moneypenny (M's secretary), the assignment delivered by M (the head of MI6, in the office with the double door), the immaculately tailored suits, the high-tech gadgets and sleek sports cars. We also learn that bearing a '00' number in the British secret service gives one license to kill: which is usually managed more with finesse than brutality, when it occurs. *Dr. No* also offers a sun-drenched Jamaican setting, Ursula Andress emerging from the sea like Botticelli's Venus in a bikini, and Joseph Wiseman as the suavely sinister villain with the truly knock-out underground compound. As a Eurasian mastermind who lost both hands in nuclear-related experiments, Wiseman has a bare minimum of screen time but his menace is felt throughout. His dastardly scheme involves interfering with the American space program, on behalf of an international network of nefarious baddies called S.P.E.C.T.R.E. (for Special Executive for Counter-Intelligence, Terrorism, Revenge and Extortion). Dr. No operates the first of many extravagantly well financed and high-tech operations that James Bond must infiltrate and disarm, usually while losing one or two local operatives on our side, but managing to save the extremely attractive young woman who is caught up in the villain's coils.

The producers of *Dr. No* followed rapidly with two equally intriguing sequels, by the same director and some of the same writing team. *From Russia with Love* has Bond teaming up with a young Russian lovely, who is under the thumb of a female operative, formerly a member of the Russian secret service, now working for SPECTRE. For exotic settings, we have a gypsy camp in Turkey, a boat chase through a Greek archipelago, and a romantic interlude in Venice. One of the action highlights is a long, and completely nonverbal, fight scene on a train between Bond and a double agent calling himself Captain Nash (performed almost entirely by the actors themselves, not stuntmen). There is also a helicopter chase which pays homage to the famous cropduster scene in Alfred Hitchcock's *North by Northwest*. Fans of 20th century theater will also be impressed by the casting. Captain Nash, Bond's impossibly cold, blond and dangerous nemesis, is played by Robert Shaw. Shaw had a good career as an actor (remembered by American audiences for his performance as Quint in *Jaws*), but he was also a distinguished writer. He wrote *The Man in the Glass Booth*, about the trial of a presumed Nazi war criminal, which had a life as a novel, a play and later a film. Rosa Klebb, the SPECTRE agent, is played by Lotte Lenya, widow of the great German composer Kurt Weill and a noted actress in her own right. She was a mainstay of Bertolt Brecht's famous Berliner Ensemble before fleeing Germany in 1933, but here is a chance to check out her *verfremdungseffekt* in a big international blockbuster. In her final scene she sports knives popping out of the toes of her shoes. Lenya said that ever afterwards, upon meeting people, she would notice their eyes stealing quickly towards her feet.

*Goldfinger* followed close upon the heels of *From Russia with Love*, and introduces a new villain, not associated with SPECTRE: Auric Goldfinger, the man with the Midas touch (played by German actor Gert Frobe). He gilds one young lady's entire body with gold, causing her death by suffocation: talk about killing a girl with kindness. Goldfinger's obsession with gold inspires him to try to invade Fort Knox – but not before trying to slice Bond, bound in an extremely vulnerable pose, in half with a laser beam (think Dr. Evil in the Austin Powers movies making the sign for quotation marks: "laaaaser beam"). We also get to meet the immortal Oddjob (played by weightlifter and wrestler Harold Sakata). Goldfinger's henchman, a solid mass of Asian muscle, does lethal things using his bowler hat as a Frisbee.

Gert Frobe's performance was dubbed, since his English was fairly minimal. *Goldfinger* was at first banned in Israel, because Frobe had been a member of the Nazi party during the Second World War. This changed when it was revealed that Frobe had been using his Nazi identity as a cover to help smuggle Jewish families out of Germany. He was disappointed that playing Goldfinger caused people to think of him as a cold villain; he was, in fact, an accomplished comic actor with a hearty laugh. (He can be seen in the family movies *Chitty Chitty Bang Bang* and *Those Magnificent Men in Their Flying Machines*.)

### TRICKY BITS:

The Bond Girls. Whether they work for the enemy and must be seduced (all in a day's work), or fall into Bond's arms as one of the perks of the job, Bond girls have silly, suggestive names and impossibly alluring looks. They are luscious and willing, and sometimes can hold their own in a fight or at a gaming table – but are hardly the feminist model we would hold up for our kids today. Again, there is many a teachable moment available. Remember that they are no more real than the rest of the fantasy world Bond inhabits: the gadgets, the cars, the exotic settings, and the effortless superiority and sangfroid of the man himself. If nothing else, you can teach your kids to distinguish between realistic drama and escapist fantasy – and that they both have their place.

## JULY

### BIOGRAPHY/MUSICAL

# Yankee Doodle Dandy

*1942, 126 minutes, black-and-white*

**Featuring James Cagney, Joan Leslie, Walter Huston, Jeanne Cagney, Eddie Foy, Jr.** *Directed by Michael Curtiz, written by Robert Buckner and Edmund Joseph*

There comes a day when fighting your way through crowds to get a good view of the fireworks just doesn't feel like a festive way to celebrate any holiday, even the Fourth of July. If watching fireworks is de rigueur for your kids, you can still introduce them to another holiday tradition that will put a smile on their face long after they've finally opted to avoid the crowds. *Yankee Doodle Dandy* is a feel-good movie any time of the year, but is especially apt now because it tells the story of one of America's greatest patriots. George M. Cohan was a song and dance man from his earliest days in vaudeville until he reigned as the king of Broadway in the 1920s and '30s. The film opens with one of his triumphant shows, in which Cohan is playing Franklin D. Roosevelt – in a musical! He is summoned to the White House to meet President Roosevelt himself, and Cohan's life unfolds in flashback as he sits in the Oval Office with FDR, wondering whether he is in trouble for representing the President on stage in tap shoes.

The grown-up Cohan is played by James Cagney, which is a treat in itself. We tend to think of Jimmy Cagney in relation to tough-guy roles, gangster films (most famously *The Public Enemy*, *Angels with Dirty Faces* and *White Heat*). So it is great fun to learn that he was a fine hoofer, and did musicals as well as dramas. In fact he started out in vaudeville, as did Cohan. In this movie Cagney does what is apparently a credible imitation of Cohan (not much film evidence remains of the man himself), with his half-talking style of singing, and his stiff-legged, loose-hipped dancing. In some numbers it looks as though Cagney's tapping owes something to the jigs and reels of Ireland, from whence both he and Cohan claimed their ancestry. This is the one performance for which Cagney received the Oscar for Best Actor, and he was proud of the film as a whole.

Another treat is watching Walter Huston, again a surprise as a song and dance man, playing Cohan's father. You may recognize his grizzled face from *The Devil and Daniel Webster* or *The Treasure of the Sierra Madre* – or you may think of him as the father of renowned director John Huston, and grandfather of actress Anjelica Huston (whom your kids might know as Morticia in the film versions of The Addams Family). Here Walter Huston is the Irish patriarch of The Four Cohans, competing for applause with his precocious son George. Young George is loaded with talent but has a knack for losing bookings for the family act, thanks to his overconfidence. The scenes in which the parents and two children perform their vaudeville acts together are delightful (Jeanne Cagney, the actor's real-life sister, plays Cohan's sister Josie). Finally, though, George strikes out on his own as a songwriter and eventually a big producer.

This is when we start to hear some famous songs, and you may find yourself exclaiming, "Oh, I didn't know it was Cohan who wrote that!" Like "Give My Regards to Broadway," "You're a Grand Old Flag" – or "Over There," the song that kept everyone's chin up during the First World War. Cohan also wrote his own adaptation of "Yankee Doodle," in which he makes the famous claim "I'm a real live nephew of my Uncle Sam, born on the Fourth of July!" (In reality Cohan was born a day or two before, but certainly adopted the Fourth of July as his own.) This number is worth it just to check out James Cagney actually dancing several feet up the proscenium arch of the theater. One wonders if this inspired the dance in *Royal Wedding* in which Fred Astaire dances up the

**Yankee Doodle Dandy** *is a feel-good movie any time of the year, but is especially apt now because it tells the story of one of America's greatest patriots.*

walls, and then keeps on going so that he's literally dancing on the ceiling.

Yankee Doodle Dandy was made during the Second World War (in fact, production started a few days before the attack on Pearl Harbor). It was meant to be a patriotic morale-booster for a nation at war, and it certainly succeeded. It is also, though, a love letter to the early greats of the American musical stage. In one scene Eddie Foy, Jr. plays his own father, Eddie Foy, the Irish-American patriarch of another family vaudeville act (Eddie Foy and the Seven Little Foys). Cagney later reprised his role as George M. Cohan in a tribute to Foy called *The Seven Little Foys*, doing a dance number with Bob Hope. The signature line from *Yankee Doodle Dandy* is a tribute to the family that hoofs together and holds on together: "My father thanks you. My mother thanks you. My sister thanks you. And I thank you."

**TRICKY BITS:**

Once again, the domestic staff tend to be African-American, including the butlers at the White House (the only position anyone at that time could imagine an African-American occupying in the White House). There is a brief shot of the Four Cohans doing a number in blackface, common in vaudeville, but it is not lingered upon. Bizarrely, even African-American performers had to use blackface makeup when presenting minstrel shows on the vaudeville circuit.

## JULY

#### DRAMA/WESTERN

# Shane

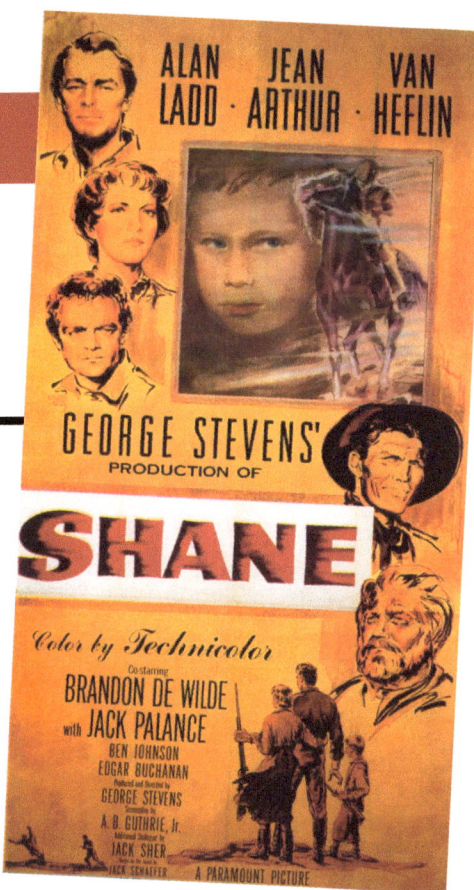

*1953, 118 minutes, color*

**Featuring Alan Ladd, Jean Arthur, Van Heflin, Brandon De Wilde, Jack Palance, Elisha Cook, Jr.** *Directed by George Stevens, written by A.B. Guthrie Jr.*

The actual heyday of the cowboys in America lasted just over a couple of decades, from the end of the Civil War in 1865 through the closing of the frontier in the late 1880s. But the heyday of the western seems to last and last, as a prism through which the country looks at its defining myths and values. Western movies have waxed and waned in popularity and quality, but they have appeared on the silver screen since it was first invented (with *The Great Train Robbery* in 1903), and so their history is as long as the history of cinema itself.

By the time George Stevens made *Shane* in 1951, the features of the genre were familiar and well established. The movie looks as if Stevens had set out to make the ultimate western, and many people think he succeeded. The story concerns one of the chief conflicts that arose on the actual frontier: between the cattle barons who wanted great expanses of land on which to feed and keep their herds, and the farmers whose settlements created fences that impeded the free movement of the cattle drives. You may remember the lyric from the musical *Oklahoma*: "Oh, the farmer and the cowman should be friends." In Shane, they most definitely are not.

Cattleman Rufus Ryker (played by Emile Meyer) wants to run all the homesteaders off his cattle range, and will stop at nothing to intimidate them into pulling up stakes. The farmers try to band together in resistance, but there is little hope for their cause until Shane rides into the disputed valley and accepts a job as a farmhand for Joe Starrett (Van Heflin). Shane's reflexes are fast, as we discover whenever there is a sudden loud noise – a souvenir of his own troubled past. But he is also cool, and Alan Ladd's blond and tawny look signals that here is the hero of the piece. He has the quiet strength needed to turn the other cheek when he is mocked as a "sodbuster" by Ryker's gang, but we can tell that this gunman who wants to walk away from violence is eventually going to have to fight. When Ryker fails to recruit Shane to work for him, he calls in reinforcements: a ruthless gunslinger named Jack Wilson, played by a dangerously smiling Jack Palance.

The inevitable confrontation between Shane and Wilson is the archetypal battle of light against dark, good against evil. The two are like titans or gods, both coming from elsewhere to protect or harm the local folk. Let's go a little further with this classical allusion, and mention the majesty of the Grand Teton range framing the drama like Mount Olympus in the background. We have a tragic messenger who comes bearing news of the death of Frank "Stonewall" Torrey (Elisha Cook Jr.) We have our own Greek chorus in the form of Joey, Starrett's young son, who connects us with Shane's humanity (he becomes a lot more human – or mortal - when he changes out of buckskin and into a farmer's blue jeans and blue shirt), and verbalizes the things that need to be said. And we have nature itself in turmoil when the drama pits characters against each other: the horses spooked in the paddock, or the storm clouds gathering over a gun duel.

This last image is one that has given many viewers occasion to wonder how deliberate George Stevens was in pursuing these classical values in the film. Was it fortuitous that dark clouds roll in just before Jack Palance and Elisha Cook Jr. face off? Or was it part of some plan? My husband had the opportunity to find out when he met

Jack Palance by chance in Berlin in 1987, when Palance was attending the Berlin Film Festival for a showing of *Baghdad Café*. They met in a hotel restaurant, and my husband popped the question about those rainclouds. Mr. Palance leaned across the table with an almost conspiratorial air and asked, "Have you ever been to Wyoming?" It turns out that every afternoon around 4:00, those clouds could be counted on to roll in over the plains and provide a rain shower. Stevens knew this and planned to shoot the scene in collaboration with nature.

It was this kind of care and deliberation that ran the production of *Shane* way over budget – and that created a movie that is impeccable, shot by shot. The filming was actually complete in 1951, a year before *High Noon* came out, but George Stevens took such time with the editing that *Shane* was not released until 1953. What was he up to? In the opening scene of the movie the character of Shane gets a long, slow entrance (remember that, very often, the more important the character the better the entrance). We see him riding from the hills, and then as he crosses the plain on his horse, we are still in the heights looking down on him from afar. Then we are at a homestead and see a deer in the foreground, its head bent down as it drinks from a flooded field, and a young boy looking at the world over his unloaded, practice rifle. The deer turns its head, and we see the figure of Shane in the background ride into the frame created by its antlers. That is what George Stevens was up to, not only in the editing but in the framing of each shot. Of the many Academy Awards for which the movie was nominated, it won for color cinematography, a tribute to the striking visual beauty of the film.

Stevens was also known for his close and sensitive work with actors (remember the performances in *I Remember Mama*). One of the threads that runs through this story is the attraction between Marian Starrett and Shane, never spoken but beautifully placed in nonverbal moments. When we first meet her, Marian is a match for her husband (a good hardworking man) in her working shirt and farm wife's pants. Gradually her femininity reasserts itself, until we see her radiant and lovely in her wedding dress, dancing with Shane at a Fourth of July gathering. Jean Arthur was coaxed out of retirement at age 50 to play the role (an inspiration in a notoriously ageist industry). She was the kind of actress directors loved: an accomplished screwball comedienne and a

woman whose inner beauty was every bit as appealing as her looks and her distinctive voice. She held her own with James Stewart in *Mr. Smith Goes to Washington*, as the kind of woman a man needs on his side. *Shane* was her last film role. Alan Ladd, at all of 5'6", was an unlikely Western hero, but his cool charisma was an ideal fit for the character of Shane. On a less than heroic note, Ladd was apparently not so adept with a gun, and Palance was no better on a horse. The one shot of bad guy Wilson mounting his horse was reportedly a shot of Palance dismounting, played in reverse.

*Shane* quotes many of the well-known elements of the western: the lone stranger passing through town on a date with his own destiny, the saloon fight, the gun duel, a funeral on the plains, a burning barn, a fistfight between friends. And one that may have been close to George Stevens' heart after his painful experiences in the Second World War: the man who is good with a gun, but knows that violence can only weary the spirit and taint the lives of everyone it touches. In that figure resides much of our fascination with westerns and our yearning for that world that maybe never existed except in imagination. It is a world in which one individual summons not only moral courage but exceptional skill and nerve, and even in the face of personal danger manages to protect us all. As that man rides away wounded, we are tempted to cry out with Joey, in the immortal final lines of the film, "Shane... Shane... Come back!"

# JULY

### COMEDY/ROMANCE/ROMANCE

## Some Like It Hot

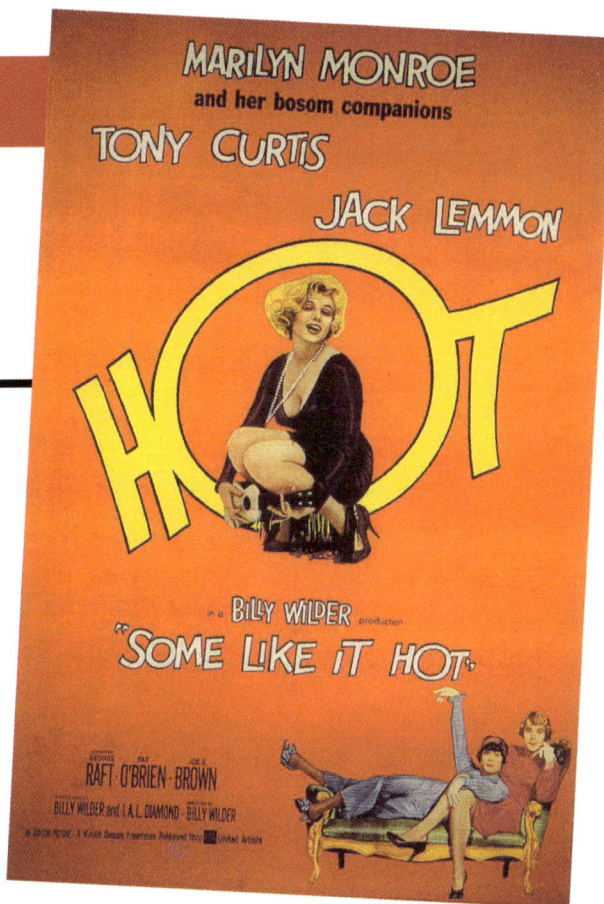

*1959, 120 minutes, black-and-white*

**Featuring Marilyn Monroe, Tony Curtis, Jack Lemmon, George Raft, Pat O'Brien, Joe E. Brown.** *Directed by Billy Wilder, written by Billy Wilder and I.A.L. Diamond*

"They just don't make them like they used to." People who say this could well be thinking of *Some Like It Hot*. With direction by Billy Wilder and a witty script by Wilder and his frequent collaborator I.A.L. Diamond, a cross-dressing comedy with some Prohibition gangsters thrown in, an all-girl band with Marilyn Monroe shimmying and crooning "boop-boop-be-doo"...no, they don't make them like this any more. Luckily they reissue them on DVD, though.

Wilder's European sensibility may explain why *Some Like It Hot* has the breathless pace and tightly wound suspense of a classic French farce. All the elements are here: dilemma, mistaken identity, danger and surprise. And the stakes are always high because our two main characters, Joe and Jerry, literally risk their lives if their disguises don't work. Joe is played by Tony Curtis (the white half of the convict pair in *The Defiant Ones*) and Jerry is Jack Lemmon (who later was paired with Walter Matthau in the movie version of Neil Simon's *The Odd Couple*). As the story begins, the friends' life looks ducky – playing together in the band of a '20s speakeasy disguised as a funeral parlor. Then they happen to witness something very like the St. Valentine's Day Massacre, and that's it for sleeping well at night. With every gangster in town looking to eliminate the witnesses, their only way out of town is disguised as members of an all-girl band headed by train to Florida. Joe becomes Josephine and Jerry is suddenly....Daphne?

The train platform offers a spectacular entrance, complete with a timely puff of steam, for Sugar Kane Kowalczyk – played by Marilyn Monroe. Marilyn is the kind of performer for whom the phrase "screen legend" was coined. Because photographs of her are everywhere in our cultural landscape, we often forget that she was an actress as well as an icon. This movie reminds us that she could be very charming and vulnerable as she played the dumb blonde (dumb like a fox), and also that she could sing and dance! (Check her out also in *There's No Business Like Show Business*, with Ethel Merman and Donald O'Connor.) Sugar has decided to get smart, for once, and find herself a nice millionaire in Florida, instead of another of the saxophone players she usually falls for. This is tough news for Joe (or Josephine), who happens to play sax – but he is not above exchanging one disguise for another and impersonating a millionaire, complete with glasses and a vocal imitation of Cary Grant, in order to win Sugar's heart.

Class and hierarchy are key elements in great comedy. The musicians are on the bottom rung, always scrambling for survival (don't forget to point this out to your kids, if they express any interest in a life in the arts!) The millionaires lining the verandah in the Florida hotel, waiting to meet showgirls, naturally are on the top. Joe E. Brown is lovely as Osgood Fielding III, who just can't help marrying one showgirl after another, and who has his eye set on "Daphne," with delightful results. Somewhere in the middle of the spectrum are the gangsters – like the artists, they will do whatever they have to in order to get by, but they have a little more financial success to show for their efforts. George Raft, a veteran tough guy, plays gangster Spats Colombo. In an earlier gangster film

*Wilder's European sensibility may explain why **Some Like It Hot** has the breathless pace and tightly wound suspense of a classic French farce.*

(*Scarface*), Raft had a character gesture of repeatedly tossing and catching a coin. He satirizes himself here by catching a coin tossed by a rival's henchman, and asking "Where did you pick up that cheap trick?"

One might speculate that Billy Wilder chose to shoot the film in black and white in order to give it a 1920s feel. In fact, it had more to do with the odd color distortions observed on the screen tests for the makeup that allowed Tony Curtis and Jack Lemmon to pass for the fairer sex. It doesn't matter – the movie certainly feels colorful enough! In a movie packed with laughs and delightful performances, one of the great pleasures is the gusto with which Jack Lemmon throws himself into his new female identity. Being courted by a millionaire turns his head a bit, with hilarious results that prepare us for the famous last line of the film. It is beautifully set up, so we won't spoil things by revealing it here. Suffice to say, it is a worthy topper for a thoroughly enjoyable, must-see film.

## JULY

### DRAMA/WAR/ADVENTURE

# The Bridge on the River Kwai

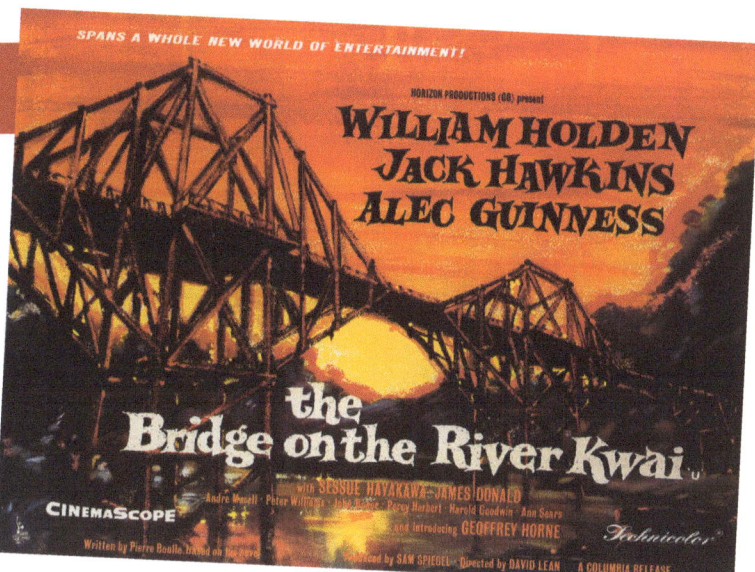

*1957, 161 minutes, color*

**Featuring William Holden, Alec Guinness, Jack Hawkins, Sessue Hayakawa, James Donald, Geoffrey Horne.** *Directed by David Lean, written by Michael Wilson and Carl Foreman, based on a novel by Pierre Boulle*

Summer is the season of the blockbuster: extra-long movies, action-packed and suspense-filled, pitting arch-nemeses against each other, often in exotic locales, peopled with stars looking to demonstrate skill with weaponry and technical gadgets, as well as the ability to plumb a hero's moral dilemma. If you think of it this way, *The Bridge on the River Kwai* is a classic summer blockbuster. There are no tights or capes, no pirates, no computer-generated monsters or cities undergoing devastation, and not much in the way of rescuing modern-day damsels hanging or falling from tall buildings. There is a titanic battle of wills between two warriors, a spectacular (real) explosion, and an action sequence so filled with tension that our 8-year-old daughter couldn't remember being so much on the edge of her seat in any movie.

There is also a setting which should probably be part of the awareness of anyone for whom a war movie suggests just battlefields and missions behind the enemy lines. The story opens in a Japanese prisoner of war camp in what is now Myanmar (then Burma), during the Second World War. The prisoners are mainly Americans, Australians and English, being used as a labor force to build a bridge linking a railway line vital to the Japanese war effort. In reality, the Japanese work on building the Burma railway cost the lives of 12,000 prisoners of war and over a hundred thousand conscripted Asian laborers. It is apt, then, that *The Bridge on the River Kwai* opens with the image of bamboo crosses lining the rail-bed, and two prisoners digging graves in the camp for the latest casualties.

If you are concerned about the length of the movie, it falls roughly into three acts, so you could certainly take a break after one of them and spread the watching over a weekend. The first act concerns the showdown between Colonel Saito, the commander of the camp, and Colonel Nicholson, the leader of a group of British soldiers who have been ordered to surrender to the Japanese. The Brits march into the camp with their military discipline fully intact, defiantly whistling the "Colonel Bogey March" – which is so catchy and so familiar, your kids will probably join in (if they've learned how to whistle). The song, originally written during the First World War, is well known for various vulgar parody lyrics, which is why it was decided to have the soldiers simply whistle it, and let the audience imagine the rest.

A clash of cultures is apparent at once. Colonel Nicholson and his officers are intent on maintaining discipline and the chain of command, refusing to allow the officers to perform manual labor alongside enlisted men. Colonel Saito presents a different argument to the new prisoners, shaped by his own culture and military code: he would have them believe that their officers have shamed them by surrendering, that they are guilty of cowardice and should express their humiliation by working side by side with the men. Military cultures may differ but we are supposed to believe (hence the controversy over Guantanamo) that the articles of the Geneva Convention must hold sway anywhere in the world. When Saito knocks Nicholson's copy of the Convention out of his hands, we know we are not in Kansas any more. Saito sets out to break Nicholson's will by ordering his officers into detention, and Nicholson locked into "the oven," a minuscule tin shack roasting under the tropical sun.

Sessue Hayakawa was nominated for the Best

*Our 8-year-old couldn't remember being so much on the edge of her seat in any movie.*

Supporting Actor Oscar for his performance as Colonel Saito. A martinet before the troops, Saito is actually a man of deep culture and refinement, who faces the necessity of committing seppuku, or ritual suicide, if this bridge project doesn't succeed. (A rarity among Asian actors of the time, Hayakawa had already achieved enormous success in Hollywood as one of the highest-paid romantic leads in the silent film era, on a par with Douglas Fairbanks and Mary Pickford and paving the way for Rudolph Valentino. As a very young man in Japan he had been groomed for a career as a naval officer and had, himself, attempted seppuku when this ambition ran aground for health reasons.) However, no enemy commander ever succeeded by underestimating the discipline, pluck and sheer grit of the British.

The role of Colonel Nicholson won Alec Guinness the Best Oscar award, and was perhaps his proudest achievement in an exceptionally distinguished career. In particular, he felt the best acting he ever did was in the scene where Nicholson is finally released from "the oven" after days of cramped privation. He modeled Nicholson's walk after the ordeal on his own son's, recovering from a bout with polio. It is equally impressive, though, to watch him gradually turn the tables on Saito and proceed to win the psychological war. Once Nicholson decides that his men's morale is suffering, as they sabotage the work efforts on the bridge, he commits to a disciplined effort to pull together and show the Japanese just what British engineering and workmanship can do. It is left to the medical officer, Major Clipton (played by James Donald), to play the necessary role of Greek chorus to this tragedy in the making. He sees clearly the madness in the mutual stubbornness of Saito and Nicholson, and then Nicholson's gradual and unconscious evolution (through ego and pride) toward collaborating with the enemy.

An alternative to the madness of military leaders confronting each other is provided by American prisoner Commander Shears. Escape from the camp is deemed impossibly dangerous because of the surrounding jungle, but Shears manages it. William Holden was cast as Shears to provide some box office appeal (not to mention eye candy). Here he plays another version of the charming bounder we met in *Sabrina*, a man for whom responsibility and discipline do not hold as much appeal as freedom and the pleasures of life. Shears is the only one of three who succeeds in the daring escape attempt and, making his way down the river, eventually finds his way to safety at an Allied military base in Ceylon. The second act of the movie largely follows the British Special Forces attempt to blackmail Shears into guiding a team back to the prison camp to blow up the bridge. Accompanying him will be the essential explosives expert Major Warden (Jack Hawkins) and a young Canadian, Lieutenant Joyce (Geoffrey Horne), who is needed because he is a strong swimmer but who may be tested as to whether he is capable of using his knife at a crucial moment.

The third and final act, which cuts back and forth between the inhabitants of the camp and the commando team making their way through the jungle toward them, is so suspenseful that you will be unlikely to want a break at this point. Nor we will spoil things for you by saying any more – except to remind you that this was before the time of computer-generated special effects. If you're hoping to see a spectacular explosion, it would have to have been real…

Director David Lean is often thought of in connection with his masterpiece *Lawrence of Arabia* (1962), but *The Bridge on the River Kwai* swept the Academy Awards every bit as impressively as the later film, with seven Oscars including Best Picture and Best Director. The award for Best Screenplay was somewhat puzzling. It was given to Pierre Boulle, the Frenchman upon whose novel the movie was based, who spoke no English. The actual screenwriters, Michael Wilson and Carl Foreman, were both blacklisted at the time and could not be given credit for their work. (The Academy eventually made it right with the two of them, Wilson posthumously and Foreman the day before he died.) In Boulle's actual experience as a prisoner of war in Thailand, a second-in-command named Saito was one of the more humane commanders in the Japanese camps, and was greatly respected by Lieutenant-Colonel Toosey, who came to Saito's defense after the war. Toosey, unlike Nicholson, quietly sabotaged rather than supported the Japanese efforts. The bridge he and his men were obliged to build actually stood for two years, until Allied bombers took it out towards the end of the war. The back story is interesting mainly in the way it points up how effectively the writers of *The Bridge on the River Kwai* drew sharply conflicting characters and created drama out of the more often excruciatingly long ordeal of trying to survive in war.

## AUGUST
### THE GREAT CLOWNS

# Silent Movie Night

What did movies do before they talked? They ran, chased, jumped, rolled, tumbled and did pratfalls. Not surprisingly, it was a golden era for physical clowning. The silent movie period produced, like any period, its masterpieces and its turkeys. The moist-eyed, slow-moving romances or costume dramas (such as are parodied in *Singin' in the Rain*) are not likely to entrance the younger members of the family, who may still be just making their peace with black and white. But anyone can find pleasure in the antics of the great clowns who got their start in vaudeville and then brought movement to the movies. Because English dialogue is not important to enjoying them, their images are famous and loved around the world: Charlie Chaplin's Little Tramp, the Keystone Cops, Buster Keaton with his pork-pie hat, and the lovable bumblers Laurel and Hardy – to mention just a few of the greats.

Introducing the family to these wonderful performers is probably best done on a grab-bag basis. This is partly because their best work is, as of this writing, inconsistently available. One can walk into an independent video store and find hundreds of Laurel and Hardy titles (where to begin??) or walk into another store and find only a few faded VHS versions of movies that might not be the ideal introduction to their magic. Some of their masterpieces are short: as in the kind of short that used to be shown before a feature-length film. Some of their feature-length films are barely longer than an hour, so it is easy to pair a full-length Charlie Chaplin movie with a couple of sublime Buster Keaton shorts, depending on what you can find.

Most of these performers bridged the transition from silent films to talkies, so you can find movies in which they speak. However, in some cases their best movies are silent, and we urge you not to shy away from those great classics. First of all, they are loaded with action, which any viewer can understand and enjoy. From time to time a few lines of dialogue or narration are required to advance the story, and they appear on the screen for a very generous length of time, enabling easy reading. If you have non-readers watching, or readers who get panicked at the pressure of reading the dialogue before it goes back to the action, our suggestion is to delegate one person who is willing to read out the dialogue card each time. (This also works for movies with subtitles.) It is not enjoyable to leave it up to chance – this usually results in silence at first, followed by everyone trying to shout out the words very quickly before the action resumes. There's enough stress already, wondering if the hero is going to be rescued from that beam at the top of the skyscraper under construction.

Why not make it fun? Pencil a few Charlie Chaplin moustaches on willing faces, maybe enlist a family member to provide some musical accompaniment (provided they have a sense of restraint), and make a BIG batch of popcorn. We are visiting the era when popcorn at the movies first became popular. Whatever you do, however, do not try these stunts at home! Buster Keaton's signature back-flip shoulder roll (dubbed a 'Buster') is something even today's physical performers can't necessarily master. Buster was a circus acrobat before he was a movie star, and he maintains his famous expressionless look (his nickname was 'The Great Stoneface') while performing the most astonishing physical feats.

**Buster Keaton** is a favorite in our house for his physical virtuosity, his surreal imagination and his deadpan innocence. (We admire these traits, as well as the impish sense of humor, in his artistic godchild Jackie Chan.) In *Sherlock Jr.* (1924, 44 minutes) Buster plays a movie projectionist who imagines a life for himself as a detective. He falls asleep and actually steps into the movie he is projecting, with wonderfully creative results. His attempts to win his girl lead him into incredible chase sequences (including flying leaps through a window in the bad guys' lair). One extraordinary scene follows another – and all in the time it would take for a contemporary hour of disposable television (minus the disposable commercials).

In *Steamboat Bill Jr.* (1928, 71 minutes) Buster wins the ultimate Freudian battle with his father, who captains a Mississippi River steamboat. Buster arrives home from college, looking to his tough father like a stuck-up, useless ponce. One wonderful "in" joke has Buster repeatedly trying on his signature pork pie hat in a store, only to have his father snatch it and toss it aside. However, one good strong storm (think winds blowing people sideways) is enough to make Buster a hero both to his girl...and his father. This movie contains the incredible scene in which the side of a house collapses on Buster, and he just happens to be standing in the opening provided by a window. Many crew members refused to be on set for this shot, as a few inches or feet in error could literally have killed Buster. (This movie was used, the same year, as an inspiration for Mickey Mouse's first talkie short, *Steamboat Willie*.)

Buster Keaton's masterpiece is considered to be *The General* (1927, 75 minutes). This is partly because Buster's extraordinary gift for comedy is wedded with his love for trains, and with a true story from the Civil War (which was not ancient history at the time the film was made). It feels like an epic film, certainly not a gag-fest. If you have train or history buffs in the family, this one is for you, as the train is virtually Keaton's co-star. Another film that is, perhaps, easier to love is *The Navigator* (1924, 59 minutes), full of ingenious nautical gags in the context of a heartfelt love story. If you must hear Buster speak, try his first talkie *Free and Easy* (1930, 92 minutes). Buster hated the film, as do many of his fans, but he does surprise everyone at the end by doing a wonderful song and dance number. Probably safer to look for his short subjects, such as *One Week* (1920, 19 minutes), where he is building a pre-fabricated house he and his bride received as a wedding gift.

**Charlie Chaplin** is a favorite all over the world, largely because of the Little Tramp character he created and featured in a number of movies. One of the most famous is *City Lights* (1931, 87 minutes), in which Charlie, dapper but down and out, romances a blind girl in the streets. It is a romantic comedy, rather than a boffo physical farce. Two of the figures that epitomize the Great Depression are the tramp and the millionaire. Chaplin is able, because his girl is blind, to be one and imitate the other. The trajectory of Chaplin's own life allowed him to inhabit both: from a Dickensian childhood in England, to the pinnacle of fame and creative power in America (followed by a long wealthy exile in Switzerland, as a result of his left-wing views.)

The little man with the good heart, the tight coat and the baggy-pants penguin walk was Chaplin's stock in trade. Sometimes the tramp character appeared in slightly different guise. In *The Gold Rush* (1925, 96 minutes) Chaplin's poor soul joins in the Klondike Gold Rush as the Lone Prospector. This movie is rich in physical gags, like the scene in which a fellow prospector appears to the hungry tramp in the guise of a chicken – an image that one can see repeated in Looney Tunes cartoons of the time. There are many great dilemmas and physical gags, including the famous one in which hardship leads him to cook his own boot and serve it up as a sumptuous feast, shoelaces and all. Sentiment slips in again, as he yearns for the attentions of a dance hall girl.

Chaplin was a believer in pantomime, and continued to make silent movies after the talkies were well established. In sticking to his guns, he made a classic with *City Lights*. The same can be said of *Modern Times* (1936, 87 minutes), his dystopian vision of a world that is changing too fast. Here inanimate objects, which are in some instances practically characters, are given sound. In

*The Great Dictator* (1940, 124 minutes), Chaplin finally speaks, toward the end of the film. He plays a Jewish barber caught up in the madness of Hitler's Germany, and then finally exploits his own physical resemblance to Der Fuehrer to create a satirical but prescient look at the evil overtaking Europe. This film was made before the United States had entered the Second World War, and stands as a testament to the humanity and social conscience Chaplin had displayed in his films all along. Paulette Godard, Chaplin's wife at the time, plays the love interest in both films.

Finally, if you can find any of the short reels by **Stan Laurel and Oliver Hardy**, be sure to include them in your evening. These two clowns were loved all over the world in their time. In Germany they were referred to as "Dick and Douf." Anyone can recognize the loving interdependence between the big know-it-all who leads the way in their interactions with the world (Hardy), and the sweet poor soul who acknowledges his own weakness with frequent tears, but who sometimes always lands on his feet (Laurel). They have been much imitated, but never rivaled. Oliver Hardy's signature move was a flirtatious look while he ruffled his tie from underneath, and the frequent exclamation "Here's another nice mess you've gotten me into!" Stan Laurel would put one hand squarely on top of his head and plump up his hair until it stood upright, while squeezing his mouth into a tight mirthless smile. These signature gestures, however, give no indication of how much variety they could wring from the contrast between them. Their films, whatever the length, display a perfect understanding of dilemma, comic timing and physical business.

Perhaps one of the best is *Scram!* (1932, 20 minutes). Mistaken identity, flouting authority, and a couple of different takes on drunkenness make this a small gem. In every short they have a wonderful shape to the plot, however improbable. Their full-length *Sons of the Desert* (1933, 68 minutes) gave its name to their international fan club. The movie is a great satire of fraternal orders (although I wonder how many fathers are Moose or Elk or Eagles nowadays). Both these movies are talkies, although Sons of the Desert doles out the gags just slowly enough, to begin with, that one is almost waiting for the dialogue cards. Still, the tale of henpecked husbands out on a spree is a wonderful introduction to the characters.

Our family favorite is *Flying Deuces* (1939, 69 minutes). It opens with Laurel despondent and wanting to drown himself for love of a Parisian beauty. Instead he and Ollie do what men who are disappointed in love are supposed to do: join the French Foreign Legion. The boys are, of course, hardly suited to military life. They find themselves having adventures in the desert, running afoul of the

authorities. In one tender scene, their escape is interrupted by a moment in the public market where they do a soft-shoe to "Shine on, shine, harvest moon." The movie ends with a reincarnation gag – remember Mr. Ed, the talking horse? Enough said.

Laurel and Hardy made silent movies as well, but there is such a wealth of their talkies available that one need not seek out the silents. While we are educating our children about the great clowns: Mack Sennett's Keystone Cops are the crazy guys one sees in full police regalia, with tall helmets and night sticks, hanging off cars and chasing bad guys with skidding turns. They had a few silent features of their own between 1912 and 1917, but mainly ended up as supporting characters in movies that featured Charlie Chaplin or Fatty Arbuckle (another irreplaceable classic clown), and eventually even Abbott and Costello. They are synonymous with bumbling incompetence, and one still sees their moves 'quoted' on screen today.

Your children should eventually get to know the iconic figures of **W.C. Fields** and **Mae West** – but as both of them professed little interest in kids, perhaps it is best to wait. Then again, if you want the whipper-snappers to get a taste of mordant grownup humor, try Fields's *Million Dollar Legs* (1932, 64 minutes), *It's a Gift* (1934, 73 minutes) or *The Bank Dick* (1940, 72 minutes). In *My Little Chickadee* (1940, 83 minutes) one gets both Fields and Mae West in a Western spoof. "Too much of a good thing is wonderful," Ms. West famously said. But you will have to be the judge, when it comes to your children.

Think of it as a treasure hunt...wherever you dig, you're likely to strike gold!

## AUGUST
### DRAMA/MUSICAL

# The Sound of Music

*1965, 174 minutes, color*

**Featuring Julie Andrews, Christopher Plummer, Eleanor Parker, Richard Haydn, Peggy Wood.** *Directed by Robert Wise, screenplay by Ernest Lehman; based on the musical with music by Richard Rodgers and lyrics by Oscar Hammerstein, book by Howard Lindsay and Russel Crouse*

The Sound of Music may be the musical we love to hate (or hate to admit we love!) but it is the quintessential "What do you mean you haven't seen - ?" movie. Whatever you may feel about it, you've got to see it. And you probably feel as though you have, if you've been subjected – as most of us have – to multiple renditions of "Climb every mountain" and "These are a few of my favorite things…" Featuring nuns and Nazis, and Julie Andrews as the über-nanny of all time, the movie has a cult following among fans (including young women and drag queens who don wimples and other costume pieces, and participate enthusiastically in "Sing-a-Long-a Sound of Music" showings in London and beyond). My husband never even saw it until the children came along, assuming for years that the various parodies of the piece summed up its virtues – wrong!

Your kids don't need to know this, however. They do need to get acquainted with one of the catchiest musical scores ever written, and a story that is as uplifting now as ever it was. The main dramatic tension line concerns the resistance of Captain von Trapp, a career officer about to be drafted into the Navy of the Third Reich, to the growing power of the Nazis which is leading toward the annexation of his native Austria. The romantic tension line concerns when the Captain, a widower, will recognize the attractive qualities in Fraülein Maria, the plainly turned-out young novice who has been given an enforced leave of absence from her convent because of her free-spirited ways, and has come to serve as governess for his seven children. Needless to say, music is an integral part of the story. It brings the lovers together, and allows their newly united family to escape from the Nazis – as did the real von Trapp family, on whom the story is based.

Captain von Trapp is played by a dashing young Christopher Plummer, one of the finest Shakespearean actors to come out of North America in the latter half of the last century (out of Canada, to be precise). His performance is subtle and wry, and utterly engaging – in spite of the fact that he has been vocal about his own reservations about the film. Maria is, needless to say, incarnated with limpid freshness by Julie Andrews. Not only is she in beautiful voice here, but she brings a comic physical awkwardness to Maria. This is in contrast to the containment and dignity that marked her previous turn as a nanny, in *Mary Poppins* the year before – so if Ms. Andrews had any anxiety about being typecast, she certainly set about creating a completely different characterization. Both characters, however, partake of Ms. Andrews' signature twinkle, which lets us know that the world will be safe for us (or even magical) if we summon our courage, our humor and our pluck. A bit of cheerful self-deprecation is also part of her toolkit. Captain von Trapp surveys with some consternation the homely brown woolen dress the young governess is wearing when she arrives at the door. When he comments upon her lack of luggage, Maria informs him that when she entered the convent she was obliged to give all her clothes to the poor. "What about this dress?" he inquires. "Oh, the poor didn't want this one!" Quite.

Maria and the Captain, in other words, "meet cute" and it takes some time before they arrive at the absolutely beautiful, simple ballad "Something Good," in which they finally reveal their feelings for one another. (Richard Rodgers wrote the lyrics as well as the music for this one song, with exceptional results.) Kids will enjoy watching the von Trapp children's attempts at hazing the new

> *My husband never even saw it until the children came along, assuming for years that the various parodies of the piece summed up its virtues – wrong!*

governess, unaware that the would-be nun has a greater sense of freedom and fun than they do. She wins their trust by playing topsy-turvy with the Captain's rules and regulations, and by prying his affections away from the stylish Baroness, played by Eleanor Parker, who longs to whisk him away on a world cruise while packing the children off to boarding school. She also nurtures their musical gifts which the Captain's friend Max Detwiler, an agent and a charming opportunist, is quick to exploit. The von Trapp Family Singers' appearance at the Salzburg Festival provides the climactic setting for a daring (and truly nail-biting) getaway, with some quietly subversive help from the nuns at Maria's old convent. The film makes for a full evening, at almost 2-1/2 hours, but is absolutely packed with comedy, romance and drama, gorgeous views of Austria, and familiar and well-loved songs by Rodgers and Hammerstein at their best. Your own family may even sing-along-a…and a sizeable dinner napkin could readily double as a wimple.

## AUGUST
### DRAMA/ROMANCE

# Casablanca

*1942, 102 minutes, black-and-white*

**Featuring Humphrey Bogart, Ingrid Bergman, Paul Henreid, Claude Rains, Sydney Greenstreet, Peter Lorre.** *Directed by Michael Curtiz, written by Julius J. Epstein, Philip G. Epstein and Howard Koch*

Is there a Top 10 film list anywhere that doesn't list *Casablanca* as a must-see film? More than just a classic, it has attained a kind of cult status among movie lovers, and has probably introduced the greatest number of famous movie quotes into our collective consciousness. While it was being made, nobody knew they were making one of the most indelible films of all time. *Casablanca* was just one of many movies Hollywood was cranking out during the Second World War, and it was rushed into the theaters a little early when North Africa was invaded in November 1942. Director Michael Curtiz had just brought *Yankee Doodle Dandy* to the screen earlier that year (reportedly with some uncredited script tweaks from Julius and Philip Epstein, who were largely responsible for the great screenplay for *Casablanca*), and this was just his next assignment. Many a Hollywood film has been ruined by the tug of war between director, producer and multiple writers – but here a serendipitous balance between romance, humor and character somehow emerged.

What is it that makes this movie so unforgettable? Well, to summon one of those oh-so-famous quotes, let's "round up the usual suspects." We'll start with Humphrey Bogart, in his first romantic role, as Rick Blaine, the owner of Rick's Café Américain in Casablanca. Until this point, Bogart had played tough guys (this is some 12 years before *Sabrina*). His Rick is also tough, until the day that the woman who broke his heart walks into his nightclub ("Of all the gin joints in all the towns in all the world, she walks into mine"). She is, of course, Ingrid Bergman at her most luminously beautiful, playing Ilsa Lund. Rick and Ilsa had been happily in love in Paris, but she deserted him suddenly and without explanation. During the course of the movie, we find out why she had to give Rick up years earlier.

As achingly romantic as the lovers' reunion is, Bogart and Bergman are hard pressed to keep the film from being stolen by Claude Rains, as the charmingly opportunist Captain Louis Renault who commands the French constabulary in *Casablanca*. Not only does he have a list of usual suspects, who can be conveniently hauled in to the police station when there is trouble, but he declares himself "shocked, shocked" to learn that there is any gambling going on at Rick's establishment – just as the croupier is bringing him his own winnings. In many ways, Claude Rains's performance epitomizes the atmosphere of the film: worldly, dangerous, unpredictable, and capable of unexpected goodness.

Paul Henreid, an Austrian actor, plays Victor Laszlo, Ilsa's idealistic Resistance leader husband who needs letters of transit to help him and Ilsa escape to Lisbon and safety. Henreid had embarked on a career as a romantic lead in Hollywood, and was concerned about playing a secondary character in *Casablanca*. He should have worried more about the stiffness of his portrayal, especially surrounded by fascinating character actors as he is. Among them are Sidney Greenstreet and Peter Lorre, who had recently appeared with Bogart in *The Maltese Falcon*. Dooley Wilson (whom we have seen in *Stormy Weather*) plays Sam, the piano player. The play on which the movie is based was inspired by a nightclub in the south of France where a black piano player entertained for a multinational clientele. Wilson is one of only three featured players in *Casablanca* born in the U.S. (and no one ever says to him "Play it again, Sam" although Rick and Ilsa both ask him to play the iconic song "As Time Goes By").

*"The problems of three little people don't amount to a hill of beans in this crazy world."*

The rich texture of the film comes partly from the fact that so many of the minor roles are played by fine European actors, real refugees from the war. Major Strasser, the top Nazi officer, is played by Conrad Veidt, who had fled Germany because his life was threatened over his anti-Nazi activities. At one crucial moment, the German officers surround Sam's piano to sing one of their old favorites from World War One, "The Watch on the Rhine." Victor Laszlo counters by signaling the band, with Rick's approval, to play "La Marseillaise," the French national anthem. One by one the patrons and staff of the Café join in, and engage in a battle of the anthems. Observers on the set said that during the shooting of this scene they saw tears in the eyes of many of the performers, who had so recently escaped from the horrors in Europe.

"We'll always have Paris," Rick tells Ilsa. But the Paris they had was one that was about to be invaded by the German army. Their love story unfolds in flashbacks of the occupation of France in 1940. For those of us whose World War II knowledge is a little creaky, the fall of France and the government based in Vichy which collaborated with the Germans, left very little safe ground in Europe. Casablanca, in North Africa, was part of unoccupied France (Morocco being, at the time, a French protectorate). This means that although there are German soldiers present, they are not in control of the city, which is still nominally under the charge of the French in the person of Captain Renault. The highly prized letters of transit, which will allow two lucky refugees safe passage to Lisbon, Portugal and the west, are a plot device rather than a historical reality.

"The problems of three little people don't amount to a hill of beans in this crazy world." So says Rick, but the writers and director know better. It is exactly because we care about the fate of these three people that we are engaged in the story, and the wartime audience for the movie was prepared to be moved by the sacrifices each of these individuals was capable of making. The screenwriters (Howard Koch as well as the Epstein brothers) won a Best Screenplay Oscar for balancing smart dialogue with heartfelt passion, and Michael Curtiz won his Best Director Oscar partly for moving the action along so dexterously that we are completely caught up in it. These are the two awards presented by the Academy in addition to Best Picture, but there is no question the cinematography, the acting and the music are equally vital to the film's unique chemistry. "Here's looking at you, kid."

**DISCLAIMER:** Our 8-year-old was shocked, shocked to learn that we were including *Casablanca* in this book. Mind you, that is because she far prefers *Key Largo*, a John Huston movie in which Bogart and a number of others take refuge in a Florida hotel in the face of a coming hurricane, where they are effectively held hostage by bad guy Edward G. Robinson. It was made in 1948, also in black and white, and is definitely a wonderful film – we recommend it. As to whether your children would enjoy it more than *Casablanca*, only you can tell. The fact is that they will encounter *Casablanca* some time, both on screen and in the multitude of references to it that everywhere abound, and we say there's no time like the present to get to know this iconic film. It repays watching again and again, so they will return to it with different eyes when they are older. Just think – it "could be the beginning of a beautiful friendship."

## AUGUST

COMEDY/MUSIC/DOCUDRAMA

# A Hard Day's Night

*1964, 87 minutes, black-and-white*

**Featuring John Lennon, Paul McCartney, George Harrison, Ringo Starr, Wilfrid Brambell, Victor Spinetti.** *Directed by Richard Lester, screenplay by Alun Owen*

# Help! COMEDY/MUSIC/FANTASY

*1965, 90 minutes, color*

**Featuring John Lennon, Paul McCartney, George Harrison, Ringo Starr, Leo McKern, Eleanor Bron, Victor Spinetti, Roy Kinnear.** *Directed by Richard Lester, story by Marc Behm, screenplay by Charles Wood*

Some twenty years ago a friend of mine reported his chagrin at overhearing one of his grade school students saying, "Did you know that Paul McCartney was in a band before Wings?" Now Wings is a musical footnote and, although Sir Paul is alive and well, many of us are obliged to ask our children "What do you mean you haven't heard of – the Beatles?!" It's a question few people in the 1960s could have imagined having to ask, when the Fab Four emerged as the greatest popular music phenomenon the world had ever seen. Legions of teenage girls pursued them, screaming and fainting at their concerts. They led the 'British Invasion' of the American musical scene, have landed more than 40 songs or records in #1 position on the charts, and have had astounding, and continuing, success throughout the world.

The generation gap has narrowed somewhat since the game Rock Band has introduced the X-Box crowd to the Beatles' infectiously catchy tunes. And it is lucky for us that, at the height of Beatlemania, the group made several movies. Few can resist the appeal of the four moptops once they see them in action. After all, few of us were able to: do you remember when the question on everyone's lips was "Who's your favorite Beatle?" This is partly thanks to the way Alun Owen, who wrote their first outing, *A Hard Day's Night*, succeeded in type-casting them. John came out as the wise-guy, Paul as the sweetheart, George as the quiet one, and Ringo as a poor soul. The foursome balanced each other as neatly as the Marx Brothers with, of course, plenty of musical talent to go along with the all the charm. One can even feel the benign blessing of the Marx Brothers on the zany antics of *A Hard Day's Night*.

Richard Lester directed these first two films, in which the Beatles play themselves. Either one of them offers an ideal way to introduce your children to the legendary group. *A Hard Day's Night* is a day-in-the-life movie, with the feel of a documentary. It starts with the lads evading a group of screaming fans, and embarking on a train trip to do a televised concert in London. (The fans in the large crowd scenes were real, but in the smaller scenes, they were cast. One young model who appears in the baggage compartment scene with the lads, Pattie Boyd, found herself living out a fan's dream: she married George Harrison.) Lester's innovative editing techniques laid the groundwork for music videos, and the antic spirit is influenced by his association with Spike Milligan of The Goon Show. Fans of *Monty Python's Flying Circus* will also recognize the permission the Pythons no doubt got from the anarchic storytelling and non sequiturs in the film

(*Monty Python's Flying Circus* started production in 1969, five years after the release of *A Hard Day's Night*). Irish actor Wilfrid Brambell plays Paul's grandfather, who comes along for the ride, and who is opportunistically amassing a collection of signed photos of the boys, clearly intended to make his fortune.

Ringo wanders away from the group for a while, the television director frets over whether the boys will show up on time, the group engage in some youthful hi-jinks, looking like nothing more than a bunch of boys who can't believe their good fortune and are playing with their newfound fame. All this larking about is pretty wholesome and fun to watch. We have gotten used to the spectacle of more recent rock bands engaging in vulgar and spoilt behavior, celebrating their fame by trashing hotel rooms and smashing their guitars on stage. It is strange to consider that the most shocking prospect the Beatles first presented was the rather shaggy haircuts, which put an end to the era of clean-cut '50s rock'n'rollers. Under the uniformity of the hair, this movie allows us to get to know the individual Beatles – and to watch them in concert, obviously enjoying the fantastic music they were playing. The movie contains classics like "She Loves You," "Can't Buy Me Love," "All My Loving," "I'm Happy Just to Dance with You," and of course "A Hard Day's Night" (based on a phrase attributed to Ringo) during the filming.

The success of *A Hard Day's Night* allowed Richard Lester, the following year, to shoot *Help!* in color. This movie has a more conventional storyline, although it still has an energy of madcap adventure. Ringo, with his trademark rings, finds one of his fingers sporting a ruby from an Eastern cult that practices human sacrifice. The next victim, the person in possession of the ring, is to be doused in red paint and sacrificed to the goddess Kaili – and Ringo can't seem to get the ring *off*. The Beatles are chased, and nearly caught, through a series of settings, from Buckingham Palace to Salisbury Plain to an Indian restaurant with a tiger in the basement (a foreshadowing of George Harrison's growing interest in eastern music). Along the way there is a fanciful "honey, I shrunk Paul McCartney" sequence. The lads are ably supported by a strong British cast, including Victor Spinetti as a scientist bent on world domination (he appeared as the highly stressed television director in *A Hard Day's Night*). Swami Clang, the head of the cult, is played by busy character actor Leo McKern (who later became very recognizable in the long-running British TV series *Rumpole of the Bailey*). Eleanor Bron provides the eye candy as Ahme, the designer-clad high priestess of the cult who is secretly working to help the Beatles.

In *A Hard Day's Night* Ringo is invited to Le Cercle, the gambling club where we first met James Bond in *Dr. No*. In *Help!* the Bond references become stronger, with locations in the Alps and the Bahamas, exotic and well-financed bad guys, gadget-obsessed scientists, sports cars, and even a trace of the Bond theme weaving through the soundtrack. The series of improbable escapes from very close calls goes on a little long ("What – again??"). But everyone seems to be having such a lark that one simply has to surrender to the silliness, and enjoy the boys. Again, we are also treated to some great classic songs, including the title number, "Ticket to Ride," "You're Going to Lose That Girl," "I Need You" and "You've Got to Hide Your Love Away." The Beatles reinvented themselves repeatedly and with great creativity – both in their music and their image. These two movies capture the early, golden age of their stardom. Their later explorations did not yield quite the cinematic success of the Richard Lester films. In 1967 the Beatles produced, directed and appeared in a one-hour TV film, called *Magical Mystery Tour*, to a fairly mixed reception. The 1968 animated film of *Yellow Submarine* does not feature the Beatles themselves (except for a brief clip), although they appear as characters. The documentary *Let It Be*, chronicling their recording sessions for the album of the same name, appeared in 1970, the year of their breakup after a decade of revolutionizing popular music together.

> **TRICKY BIT:**
>
> Political correctness would make it unlikely for a cult of buffoonish Eastern types devoted to human sacrifice to make it into a contemporary film, no matter how irreverently played for laughs. It was also the norm in this period, and for some time afterwards, to cast white English actors in the role of East Indian characters (think Alec Guinness in *A Passage to India*). In the bad old days, awareness of the Indian immigrants in England was restricted to the fact that they ran the only restaurants where one could find decent food in London. Now South Asian artists living in Britain are receiving knighthoods for their achievements. And it is easier to find good food of many varieties in London.

## AUGUST
### DRAMA

# To Kill a Mockingbird

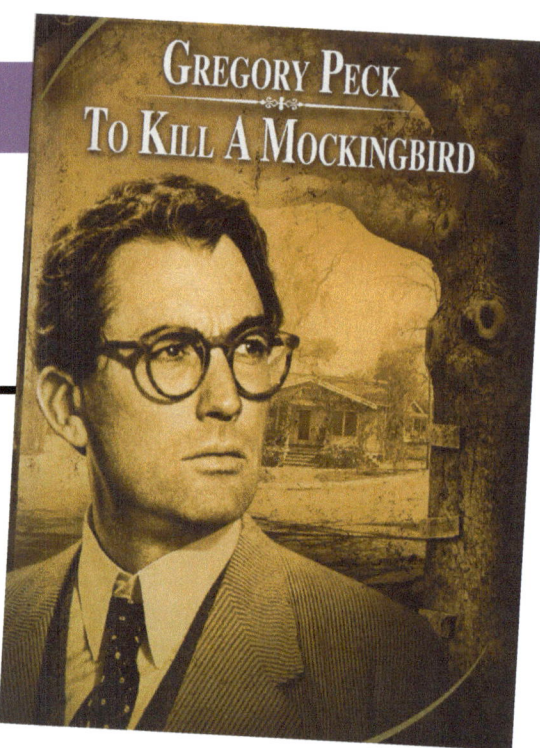

*1962, 129 minutes, black-and-white*

**Featuring Gregory Peck, Mary Badham, Phillip Alford, Frank Overton, Brock Peters, Robert Duvall, Collin Wilcox, James Anderson, Estelle Evans, John Megna.** *Directed by Robert Mulligan, screenplay by Horton Foote, based on the book by Harper Lee*

For this great, must-see American classic, let's begin with a **Tricky Bit**. Growing up in Canada, I had certainly heard of *To Kill a Mockingbird*, but never saw the movie and was never assigned the book to read in school. It is certainly a "what do you mean you haven't seen" kind of film, but I was concerned about showing it to our children because I had heard it concerns a black man unjustly accused of raping a white girl. That seemed a subject better saved until they were a little older. But the movie has been an important part of the viewing lives of so many American friends, we decided to watch it as a family and just be prepared to explain where necessary. As it turns out, the subject is handled so tactfully that it becomes entirely secondary to the absorbing elements of the film. Afterwards I asked our 8-year-old daughter, "What do you understand the word 'rape' to mean?" Her reply was "Harassing a girl and doing things she doesn't want." That definition seemed mercifully appropriate to her age, as well as entirely adequate for appreciating the story. (Especially as the evidence suggests that no rape actually did occur.)

Atticus Finch, the lawyer hero of this tale, famously says "You never really understand a person until you consider things from his point of view – until you climb into his skin and walk around in it." This movie offers many opportunities to consider things from different people's point of view. It is especially riveting for kids because the story is seen from a child's perspective. We hear the voice of a grown-up Jean-Louise Finch, or "Scout," narrating as she remembers the events from the perspective of maturity, but we experience them the way the young Scout does: the scary house on the corner and its mysterious inhabitants, the grown-up concerns overheard while the kids are in bed, the frustration of not being tall enough to see through the window into the courtroom or over people's heads when important things are happening. When Scout's brother Jem is asked to sit up while Scout sleeps and his father drives the housekeeper Calpurnia home, the shadows of leaves on the porch shake ominously, the cry of night birds is especially loud and harsh, and the porch swing at the Radleys' house seems to move of its own accord. The opening image of the film is a cigar box full of a child's discovered 'treasures' and a crayon tracing the title while a child hums. Elmer Bernstein's elegiac musical score starts from the notes that a child might pick out on a piano on a lazy afternoon, but swells with menace when the children are out at night on a heart-pounding adventure.

There is even an opportunity for children watching this movie to climb into their parents' skins for a bit. Many of us grew up in neighborhoods where, like the Finch children, we were allowed to walk alone through the woods or roam free after dark, occupying ourselves as we pleased until the door of our house opened and we were called in for dinner or for bed.

Most important, of course, is the point of view of each of the residents we meet in the "tired old town" of Maycomb in 1932. The movie takes us from one hot, late summer day through an entire school year, another summer and into the autumn, in a small southern town feeling the weight of both the Great Depression and racial segregation. Early on we meet Walter Cunningham, a farmer who is paying Atticus for his legal services by delivering a bag of hickory nuts to the Finch home, since he has no money. When Scout later spots Cunningham in a crowd of men outside the town's jail in the middle of the night, she speaks sympathetically to him about his "entailment" (the debt against his land that would prevent him from fully owning it). Her innocent kindness shames him, but also prevents a tragedy. Does the pain of poverty and struggle excuse the racism that leads these men to band together in inhumanity? No. But neither does the story flatten the characters and allow us to demonize them.

We could easily demonize white girl Mayella Ewell for bringing false accusation against Tom Robinson (Brock Peters), a decent black man with a family. Before we arrive in the courtroom, though, we get a picture of what Mayella's life might be like. Earlier in the movie, we have seen Atticus called out of his house, with a long unused rifle, to shoot a mad dog that is staggering down the street. In the very next scene he pays an evening visit to Tom Robinson's wife and family. Bob Ewell, Mayella's father, appears out of the darkness to confront Atticus. We see Ewell in the road, bottle in hand, staggering and (we can almost imagine) foaming at the mouth just like the mad dog we have seen. Alcoholism and violence are the realities in the Ewell home that underlie Mayella's behavior.

The story's most memorable example of shifting one's point of view is the redemption of Boo Radley. Robert Duvall, in his first screen appearance, makes Boo's haunted shyness approachable for the children who have long imagined him as a bogeyman. In keeping with a world in which characters are called Atticus and Calpurnia, and the ancient virtues of civility and respect for the law are held dear, the storytelling takes an approach from the classic Greek theater. Violent and tragic moments are reported rather than shown. The one exception is something the children experience, Jem and Scout's perilous walk home from the Halloween party. But again, since we see the action largely through Scout's eyes (obscured by a ridiculous ham costume), we do not witness the events directly.

The retelling of violent events, especially from different points of view, is what provides the tension in courtroom drama – and this one is one of the best. The beauty of Atticus Finch's eloquence in the trial scene has inspired many a young person to make a career in the law. The character of Atticus is lovingly drawn (perhaps because he was based on the father of Harper Lee, who wrote the novel). It is his skin we would most like to climb into and walk around in, because it is clear that from that perspective we would see every living creature, from a man to a mockingbird, with equal respect. He is the gentlest, most reasonable father imaginable, allowing

> *The subject is handled so tactfully that it becomes entirely secondary to the absorbing elements of the film.*

his children to "act out" a little by calling him Atticus rather than 'dad' or 'father' – an unheard-of liberty in those times. He is a perfect gentleman to Calpurnia, the black housekeeper who acts almost as a mother to his children (their actual mother having died some years earlier). And he is the strongest advocate we could imagine for integrity and common decency. The respect in which Atticus Finch holds others is mirrored by the respect in which he is held. In one moving moment of the film, Atticus prepares to leave the courtroom after the trial. The Reverend Sykes, watching from the gallery with Atticus's children, says "Jean Louise. Jean Louise, stand up. Your father's passing."

The character of Atticus Finch found his ideal embodiment in Gregory Peck. Rarely have an actor and a role been so well matched. Respected through a long career by audiences and peers alike, Peck often said that Atticus Finch was his favorite role. Many of the people involved with the movie spoke of it as a highlight in their careers. Peck and his family formed long friendships with Harper Lee, the novelist, and the actress Mary Badham (whom Peck always called "Scout"). Brock Peters, who gave a heartfelt performance as Tom Robinson, also remained friends with Peck and spoke the eulogy at his funeral. Not only in the Oscar-winning achievements of Horton Foote's screenplay, Peck's performance and the art direction, the movie shows the great love and care that were poured into it by all who were part of it.

**MORE TRICKY BITS:**

**Bob Ewell calls Atticus a "nigger-lover" and the "n word" appears elsewhere. Ewell also calls grown African-American men "boy." Since racism is a subject of the story, it is strongly depicted in all its ugliness.**

## SEPTEMBER
### MUSICAL/ROMANCE

# My Fair Lady

*1964, 170 minutes, color*

**Featuring Audrey Hepburn, Rex Harrison, Stanley Holloway, Wilfrid Hyde-White, Gladys Cooper, Jeremy Brett, Theodore Bikel.** *Directed by George Cukor, written by Alan Jay Lerner, based on a play by George Bernard Shaw, songs by Alan Jay Lerner and Frederick Loewe*

Possibly the greatest musical ever written? We're not alone in thinking so. The stage version of *My Fair Lady* was a long-running smash hit in New York and London, and the film won 8 of the 12 Oscars it was nominated for. Definitely on our desert island list of films we could see over and over again… Clocking in at almost 3 hours, the movie offers an old-fashioned intermission in the middle, complete with orchestral interlude, and it certainly makes a convenient spot to take a break if you prefer to spread the pleasure over two nights of watching. You may, however, be reluctant to stop at the intermission as there is almost never a moment that is less than funny, colorful and rich.

The first ingredient in an impeccable film is the script. Alan Jay Lerner had the great good sense to lean heavily on the original play, *Pygmalion* by the brilliant British playwright George Bernard Shaw. Lerner's lyrics, coupled with Frederick Loewe's memorable melodies, rise organically from the action with a wit that Shaw himself would have approved. He would not have approved of the hint of romance that *My Fair Lady* allows into the relationship between Professor Henry Higgins and his protégé Eliza Doolittle…but this is a musical, after all. And the romance is handled with such irony and restraint that it never slackens into the kind of syrupy stuff that would have violated Shaw's bracing spirit of truth.

The setting is London in the Edwardian era (as we are reminded in *Mary Poppins*, "the age of men"). A pair of gentlemen, confirmed bachelors with a shared interest in phonetics, take on the project of turning a Cockney flower girl into a lady. It looks like a Cinderella story for Eliza Doolittle, who is plucked from the street with dirty face and dirty clothes, and turned into a virtual princess (at least, the men are able to pass her off as a princess at the embassy ball). But Shaw's social consciousness never allows us to forget that a girl who is dragged from one class into another has no real identity or future, besides marriage with some idle and neglectful toff. Professor Higgins and his pal Colonel Pickering are, in the assessment of Higgins's mother, nothing more than "a pair of great babies playing with their live doll." Their civilized charm is balanced with complete self-satisfied blindness, and we are rooting for Eliza when she finally flings Higgins's slippers at him and begins to stand up for herself.

Class is very visible in this world – and audible. Simply by opening their mouths to speak, the English betray their origin and their social standing. Henry Higgins, in a kind of Sherlock Holmes parlor trick, can place someone's birthplace within a mile, simply based on the sound of their vowels. As he says (or rather speak-sings) to Pickering, upon meeting Eliza selling violets outside Covent Garden, "If you spoke the way she does, instead of the way you do – why, you might be selling flowers too." Alan Jay Lerner wanted a great actor in the role of Higgins, rather than a great singer. One certainly applauds his choice as Rex Harrison patters his way through great questions such as "Why can't the English teach their children how to speak?" and "Why can't a woman…be more like a man?"

Harrison is the perfect embodiment of the English cad: supremely well-spoken, urbane and self-confident, maddeningly insensitive…and irresistibly appealing. It is simply devilish the way he drily sends up his own piggishness, while at the same time embracing it with gusto, making him *the* Higgins to haunt any other actor

> *Jack Warner got what he wanted: a bona fide, radiantly beautiful movie star, whose fairy tale transformation truly takes one's breath away.*

who attempts the role. (Seth MacFarlane, creator of the animated TV series *Family Guy*, has said that the character of the dastardly baby Stewie, who inexplicably speaks with an English accent, is meant to be a sort of "evil Rex Harrison.") He is somewhat balanced by Wilfrid Hyde-White's Colonel Pickering, who has the old-school manners without the arrogance. Audrey Hepburn's Eliza convincingly traces the struggle of undergoing a makeover so extreme she has to re-learn how to speak, much less what to speak about. Hepburn's casting in the role was somewhat controversial, as many thought it should have gone to Julie Andrews, who originated the role onstage with Rex Harrison. Further, much of her singing in the film wound up being dubbed by Marni Nixon, to Hepburn's disappointment. (An exception is the early, angry verses of "Just You Wait, 'Enry 'Iggins," which is delicious and pure Audrey.) But producer Jack Warner got what he wanted for the role: a bona fide, radiantly beautiful movie star, whose fairy tale transformation truly takes one's breath away.

Stanley Holloway, the delightful English character actor, did get tapped from the stage production to play the role of Eliza's father, the dustman Alfred P. Doolittle. He practically steals the show, with his original moral viewpoint and the great production number "Get Me to the Church on Time." A young Jeremy Brett, looking dewy and fresh as Freddy Eynsford Hill, also gets a famous number, "On the Street Where You Live." It is fascinating to see this actor, who aged into an indelible Sherlock Holmes in the Granada Television series shot in the 1980s and early '90s, appearing here as a young romantic lead. Gladys Cooper is lovely as the no-nonsense Mrs. Higgins, who absolutely has her son's number. (Upon meeting Henry unexpectedly at Ascot, Mrs. Higgins offers a most unsentimental, "Henry! What a disagreeable surprise.") Theodore Bikel shows up in a character turn as Zoltan Karpathy, a former student of Higgins, who has the audacity to put Liza to the test at the embassy ball and who, by virtue of being foreign (Hungarian, no less!), is naturally assumed to be slippery and "clever."

Director George Cukor was famous for coaxing wonderful performances from actors through his long career, as he certainly did here. The film is visually lush and rewarding as well. The producers insisted on shooting the film entirely in the studio rather than on location, but this allowed the extraordinary production design team to create a cozy, insular world that fits Professor Higgins like a glove. The camera lingers lovingly over Cecil Beaton's stunning black and white costumes for the Ascot horse race, where Eliza gets her first 'test run' as a lady, with hilariously mixed results. In the original Greek myth underlying the story, the sculptor Pygmalion falls in love with the statue of a woman he has created. Higgins is unable to admit falling in love with Eliza, and can only go so far as to acknowledge "I've grown accustomed to her face." However, we would have to have marble hearts not to fall in love with the entire film.

## SEPTEMBER

DRAMA/ROMANCE

# Rebel Without a Cause

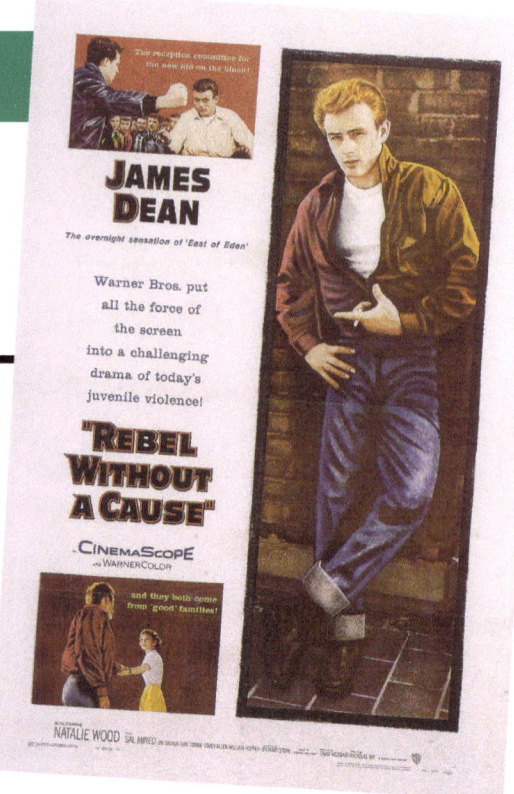

*1955, 111 minutes, color*

**Featuring James Dean, Natalie Wood, Sal Mineo, Jim Backus, Ann Doran, Dennis Hopper.** *Directed by Nicholas Ray, screenplay by Stewart Stern*

"School days, school days, dear old golden rule days..." *Rebel Without a Cause* is not the kind of movie that will make you feel great about starting a new school year – but it will introduce you to the legendary James Dean. Images of James Dean often keep company with those of Marilyn Monroe: two beautiful, luminous stars, doomed to die young. As with Marilyn, the iconic status often overshadows the very real talent. In *Rebel Without a Cause*, the second of the three films in which Dean had a starring role, he hits his marks and delivers a deeply felt and convincing portrait of troubled teenager Jim Stark.

We sometimes look back at high school in the '50s through a sentimental haze: bobby socks, poodle skirts, school dances, tough guys who aren't really all that tough (*Grease, Peggy Sue Got Married*...). This movie, made in the middle of the '50s, focuses on the grittier concern of juvenile delinquency. *Rebel Without a Cause* appeared in the same year as *Blackboard Jungle* – they are the west coast and east coast takes on the issue. The opening scene of *Rebel* introduces the three main characters in a police station, each of them in trouble. But they are all basically good kids, trying to stay connected with parents who just don't get it. The movie starts as a high school drama and ends like a Greek tragedy. In the plays and myths of ancient Greece, the family is always at the center of the drama. Here the American family, and the way it can sometimes fail its children, is laid bare.

Jim Stark is starting the year at a new high school, having been moved unwillingly from another community. There is an implication that the family has to keep moving because Jim gets into trouble, but the parents fail to acknowledge that their own persistent quarreling might be a factor in his tormented behavior. Jim's father is unable to hold his own with his critical wife – the apron he wears through one long scene pretty much tells the story. "You're tearing me apart!" Jim famously cries, caught between his warring parents and looking for some help and understanding with his own problems. Jim Backus, usually cast in comic roles, plays Jim's father. The casting allows him to draw on the ineffectual qualities he displayed as the voice of cartoon character Mr. Magoo, while struggling to become the father his boy needs.

It is never easy to be the new kid in school. Jim tries to strike up a conversation with his neighbor Judy (played by Natalie Wood), who was in the police station the night before for breaking her curfew. It turns out, though, that Judy hangs out with a tough crowd who are not at all interested in having Jim fit in. A school trip to the planetarium ends with a switchblade fight and a challenge to a "chickie run" with Butch Gunderson, the head of the gang. This involves taking stolen cars and driving them off a cliff into the ocean. The first driver to jump clear from his car is labeled a chicken. The very fact that Jim shows up seems to raise Butch's estimation of him, and it seems as though the two could actually become friends. But Butch's sleeve gets caught on the handle of his door and, even though he tries to bail out of his car first, he doesn't succeed.

This isn't the only tragic friendship Jim gets involved in. Classmate John 'Plato' Crawford (played by Sal Mineo) looks up to Jim and becomes very attached to him. Although nothing explicit is stated, the attachment has a

*Dean delivers a deeply felt and convincing portrait of troubled teenager Jim Stark.*

romantic feeling, just as Jim is becoming romantically drawn to Judy. Each of the three teenagers is yearning for a family. Judy is being rejected by her father because she still longs to be close and affectionate with him, while he obviously finds her budding womanhood threatening. 'Plato' has been abandoned by his rich parents, his only friend and ally the African-American housekeeper who looks after and obviously cares for him. When the kids break into an abandoned mansion together one night, the fantasy life they find themselves acting out is that of an intact and happy family.

Jim Stark's iconic red jacket is part of director Nicholas Ray's strong visual approach and expressionistic use of color in the film. In one scene James Dean and Natalie Wood are bathed in color, blue in one side of the frame and red in the other, like a pair of Plato's mismatched socks. Ray attained cult status among European directors, and this bold visual look is familiar from many succeeding "art" films – or to anyone who regularly watches the television program *Smallville*. Originally drawn to architecture, one can also see Ray's eye for the power of a building in the way he uses the planetarium in the final scene, like a Greek temple with a tragedy unfolding on its steps.

An aura of tragedy surrounds *Rebel Without a Cause* partly because each of its three young stars was marked for early death. James Dean famously perished in a car accident, at the age of 24, shortly after shooting his role in *Giant* but before the movie could be released. In an incredible telescoping of his career, Dean was nominated for an Academy Award in 1956 for his first picture, *East of Eden*. He was already dead, and went on to win a second posthumous nomination the following year for the work in his third picture, *Giant*. Sal Mineo, only 16 when he gave his Oscar-nominated performance as Plato, was stabbed to death in the street at the age of 37 (giving a grim resonance to his own nickname, "The Switchblade Kid"). Natalie Wood, whose career began early with an appearance as the little girl in *Miracle on 34th Street* and included the poignant role of Maria in *West Side Story*, drowned off Catalina Island at the age of 43, thereby breaking many a heart.

**TRICKY BITS:**

Many of the behaviors the characters engage in come with a strong "do not try this at home" warning on them. Public drunkenness, staying out late at night, knife fights, dangerous driving, breaking and entering, bullying, and discharging firearms…those darn kids! At the same time, the main question the film poses is: how can young people who are basically good get into so much trouble? The answer should be a reassuring one for parents, at the same time that it challenges us to be alert, present and available. The teenagers in the film may look like young adults, but they deeply need guidance and love, and closeness with their families. The movie gives kids permission to acknowledge how confusing and overwhelming life can be – at the same time allowing us to point out that driving a car off a cliff is not the ideal response. After seeing the film, though, at least you will know why Marty McFly, the father of Michael J. Fox's character in *Back to the Future*, can't stand to be called "chicken."

## SEPTEMBER

### DRAMA/WESTERN/ADVENTURE

# The Treasure of Sierra Madre

*1948, 126 minutes, black-and-white*

**Featuring Humphrey Bogart, Walter Huston, Tim Holt, Bruce Bennett, Barton MacLane, Alfonso Bedoya, John Huston.** *Directed by John Huston, screenplay by John Huston, based on a novel by B. Traven*

The Treasure of the Sierra Madre is a must-see film, if only so that you can finally hear the original version of those much-quoted, misquoted and parodied lines about not needing any stinking badges. A group of Mexican bandits, led by a man named Gold Hat with a wide and cynical grin, try quite implausibly to pass themselves off as *federales* (or government troops). When challenged to show their badges, we get the famous reply "Badges? We ain't got no badges. We don't need no badges. I don't have to show you any stinking badges." So there you go.

Set in Mexico, this was one of the first Hollywood movies to be shot on location outside the U.S. Each beautifully composed shot tells the story – much of the time you could turn off the sound and still follow what's going on. Director John Huston also wrote the screenplay, based on a novel by the elusive writer B. Traven. He cast his father, Walter Huston, as the old timer Howard – and got him to play the role without his false teeth. Walter Huston had a long and distinguished career of his own (we saw him as a song and dance man, playing George M. Cohan's father in *Yankee Doodle Dandy*, and he also famously played Scratch in *The Devil and Daniel Webster*). This made for a bit of Oscar history when both father and son won for *The Treasure of the Sierra Madre*: Walter for Best Supporting Actor and John for both screenplay and direction. John had successfully ignored the urgent messages coming to the location from the studio on another point: based on the footage they were seeing, the executives were afraid that Walter Huston was stealing the movie from its star, Humphrey Bogart.

Bogart was at this time Hollywood's top male actor, partly as a result of his breakthrough role in *The Maltese Falcon* in 1941 – his previous collaboration with John Huston. One of the pleasures of *Sierra Madre* is getting to watch the usually cool Bogart descend into chuckling madness, wild-eyed with paranoia and greed. However, the beauty of the script is that it does not tell the story of greedy men learning a lesson. This is a moral tale, not a moralistic one. Greed is one of the archetypal seven deadly sins, and in each of us lies the potential for its seeds to grow. The three men who go prospecting for gold in the mountains of the Sierra Madre are good, honest and fair men. At first.

Down and out in Tampico, Mexico, Fred C. Dobbs (Bogart) is first seen panhandling. He is sufficiently ashamed of himself that he doesn't look directly at a well-dressed American tourist when he asks, "Say, buddy, can you stake a fellow American to a meal?" The result is that three times in the same day he approaches the same man, in a cameo played with some relish by John Huston. Dobbs is certainly willing to do an honest day's work. He and fellow American Bob Curtin (Tim Holt) sign on to work for an oil rigger hiring temporary help (Barton MacLane). When he cheats them of their wages, they find him in a bar and give him a good beating. But from the boss's wallet, stuffed with cash, they take only what they are owed: no more and no less.

The two men meet Howard (Walter Huston), an experienced prospector, in a flophouse. Howard is a bit of an oracle. He predicts everything that can and will happen if they pool their resources and go looking for gold in the mountains. This includes his prophetic assessment of the bandits in the hills, "They'll kill you for your shoes." But not even Howard can resist the urge to try once again to find that vein of gold. As he tirelessly leads the younger men into rough terrain, we hear Dobbs's muttered complaint that they have signed on to follow a mountain goat. Howard's gleeful jig when they hit pay dirt is a classic cinema moment.

The quest for gold that united the three men gradually drives them apart. Howard and Curtin each find a different kind of treasure than they were seeking. But the fate of Fred C. Dobbs is full of such brutal irony that it gives rise to another famous cinematic moment: his two prospecting partners giving themselves up to uncontrollable laughter at the joke the cosmos has played on them all. If the movie has a point to make, it is that treasure comes in many forms that don't always look like a sack of gold dust. Sometimes it looks like a great story, well told, that stands the test of time.

> *One of the pleasures of* **Sierra Madre** *is getting to watch the usually cool Bogart descend into chuckling madness, wild-eyed with paranoia and greed.*

## SEPTEMBER
### COMEDY/CRIME/THRILLER

# The Ladykillers

*1955, 91 minutes, color*

**Featuring Alec Guinness, Cecil Parker, Herbert Lom, Peter Sellers, Danny Green, Jack Warner, Katie Johnson.** *Directed by Alexander Mackendrick, written by William Rose*

Most American families will recognize Sir Alec Guinness as the older Obi-Wan Kenobi in *Star Wars*, a role that made him a huge international star. It was a source of chagrin for Sir Alec that he became so associated with a relatively small role in a science fiction epic, overshadowing a long and distinguished career on both stage and screen. Even before he played serious roles in such major movies as *Bridge on the River Kwai, Lawrence of Arabia* and *Doctor Zhivago*, Guinness was known for his incredible versatility in the Ealing Studio comedies produced in England after the Second World War.

*The Ladykillers* is one of the best of these. It is a dark comedy, to be sure, but one in which innocence triumphs over wrongdoing. Innocence takes the form of Mrs. Wilberforce, the definitive little old English lady, frail-looking and a little dotty. (The delightful actress, Katie Johnson, was originally denied the part because the producers thought, at 77, she might be *too* frail. However, the younger actress they cast died before filming could begin, and so Johnson got to strike a blow against ageism and play the role.) She is a regular visitor at the local police station, bearing tales of strange occurrences in the neighborhood – like the UFO sighting her neighbor reported which, she's oh so sorry, was probably something else entirely. The police smile and nod indulgently. Humoring eccentric old ladies is all in a day's work for a British bobby.

Mrs. Wilberforce shares her house with a parrot named General Gordon (whom she and her friends seem to resemble). General Gordon is her sole housemate until a mysterious man arrives at the door, in answer to her ad looking for a lodger. It is "Professor" Marcus, or Alec Guinness sporting a mop of stringy hair and made up to emphasize all the worst claims about British dentistry. Of course, Mrs. Wilberforce is delighted to learn that the professor and his 'associates' want the room primarily for rehearsals of their string quintet. They arrive with violin and cello cases, which in heist movies are favored storage places for weaponry. And, indeed, none of Professor Marcus's gang can actually play a note. They put on a phonograph record of Boccherini's String Quintet in E to mislead Mrs. Wilberforce, while they plan a daring robbery of King's Cross Station.

The "Professor's" gang of gentlemen criminals turn out to be more gentlemen than criminals. They use Mrs. Wilberforce as an unsuspecting accomplice in the meticulously planned and hilarious robbery, and it looks as though they are set to get away with it – until, through a marvelous moment of bungling by the "cellist," she discovers the "lolly" and realizes what her boarders have been up to. Mrs. Wilberforce threatens to go to the police, so the gang concludes that they have no choice but to kill her. This bumbling crew may think of themselves as master criminals, but not one of them is keen on bumping off a sweet, innocent lady, so they draw straws for the job. Would-be ladykillers, they succeed only in knocking one another off, in increasingly ludicrous fashion. The police, of course, are not too persuaded by Mrs. Wilberforce's story of recovered loot, and so all's well that ends well.

The gang features the usual assortment of characters offering qualities from ruthlessness to brute strength. Two of its members, Peter Sellers and Herbert Lom, later achieved fame as Inspector Clouseau and Chief Inspector Dreyfus in the Pink Panther series. Peter Sellers became

*Skilled actors, brilliant writing and impeccable direction combined with a delicious sense of social satire.*

famous for his versatility (playing three different roles in Stanley Kubrick's *Dr. Strangelove*). Perhaps he was inspired by the company he kept at Ealing Studio. Alec Guinness played no fewer than eight roles (all members of the same aristocratic family) in the 1949 comedy *Kind Hearts and Coronets*. If you find yourself drawn to the dry British crime comedy, it is definitely worth a look, as is another of the Ealing Studio highlights, *The Lavender Hill Mob* (1951), which features Guinness again with Stanley Holloway (Eliza Doolittle's father in *My Fair Lady*).

The Coen Brothers remade *The Ladykillers* in 2004, moving the setting to the American South, where one might presumably still find gentlemen thieves and righteous old ladies capable of thwarting them. But there is no match for the British when they satirize themselves. Politeness, proper behavior and class consciousness can put a crimp in a criminal's style, and it is great fun to see the conflict within each of the original characters. It is the same conflict that drives the antics of the Monty Python crew, among others. Skilled actors, brilliant writing and impeccable direction combined with a delicious sense of social satire: these are hallmarks of the Ealing Studio comedies. And when John Cleese needed the perfect director to helm his 1988 comedy *A Fish Called Wanda*, he called an Ealing veteran out of retirement, Charles Crichton of *The Lavender Hill Mob*.

# OCTOBER
### COMEDY/DRAMA/ROMANCE

## Sullivan's Travels

*1941, 90 minutes, black-and-white*

**Featuring Joel McCrea, Veronica Lake, Robert Warwick, William Demarest, Franklin Pangborn, Porter Hall.**
*Written and directed by Preston Sturges*

Hollywood and the Great Depression in many ways go hand and hand. The golden era of the Hollywood studios began shortly before the stock market crash of 1929. While unemployment, bread lines and deprivation were searing our parents' and grandparents' psyches, the silver screen was populated with screwball comedies and extravagant Busby Berkeley musicals. This phenomenon is at the heart of the argument that the entertainment industry is recession-proof. When times are tough, people need to escape their reality into dreams of glamour and success.

*Sullivan's Travels* takes a satiric look at just these issues – and it is a fun-filled ride. The title tips its hat to 'Gulliver's Travels' by Jonathan Swift, and hints to us that we should be on the lookout for satire and fantasy. Joel McCrea plays John L. Sullivan, a Hollywood film director who is simply too successful to be believed. He has become rich on movies like "Ants in Your Plants 1938," movies which make Busby Berkeley's glossy fluff look serious. However, Sullivan's soul yearns for art. Rather than delivering feel-good products that make money for his fawning producers, he wants to make a serious, gritty film of hard knocks entitled "O, Brother, Where Art Thou?" (Those who enjoyed the 2000 Coen Brothers film of that name will be gratified to see that Sullivan's Depression movie was finally made…with tongue held firmly in cheek.)

Sullivan decides to set out on the road as a hobo, and rack up some experiences of suffering that will help him become a Serious Artist. However, he just can't seem to get away from the caravan of vehicles ready to tend to his every need – and every time he takes a wrong turn he winds up back in Tinseltown. In the middle of one night he meets Veronica Lake in a diner on the outskirts of Hollywood. She is a failed actress trying to get home with her dignity intact, and he is a hopeless Hollywood insider trying to achieve escape velocity. Fortunately, she buys his down-and-out disguise, and they set out on the road together as a pair of hobos. For Veronica Lake to appear as a poor girl who couldn't make it in Hollywood is, in itself, worth a wry smile. She was a legendary poster girl, whose cascade of blonde hair over one eye is iconic (its echo can be seen in the redheaded coif of the ultimate animated screen siren, Jessica Rabbit in the 1988 Robert Zemeckis film *Who Framed Roger Rabbit*).

The movie looks as though it is headed for a happy romantic ending, with Sullivan accepting the great good fortune that always seems to attend upon his life. Then suddenly it veers into more serious territory. Sullivan sets out to quietly and anonymously distribute $5 bills to the needy people he has encountered on the streets. Through a series of mishaps and mistaken identity, he finds himself not only truly down and out but actually arrested and placed in a prison chain gang. We are not sure how he is going to find his way back this time, as he is experiencing the real hardship and injustice of the underprivileged, not the picturesque variety he had been looking for. One evening the prisoners are invited to a movie screening at a local church. The scene is notable partly because the

*When times are tough, people need to escape their reality into dreams of glamour and success.*

African-American minister and congregation are presented with great dignity, as they extend their generosity to those less fortunate: the ragged, ravaged band of mostly white prisoners. The movie they are showing is a cartoon and, as he watches the faces of prisoners and parishioners roaring with laughter, Sullivan realizes what he failed to understand before. In hard times, people need to laugh.

That is something Hollywood understood during the "Dirty Thirties" and we have many fine comedies and musicals to cherish because of it. *Sullivan's Travels* successfully straddles the two sides of the period: the glamour and the hardship. If your family is ready for a more serious look at the Depression, the must-see film is *The Grapes of Wrath*, based on John Steinbeck's powerful novel of the same name. This might well be the movie that John L. Sullivan dreamed of making. When *The Grapes of Wrath* appeared in 1940, the producers advertised that no tickets would be sold to children. This is not because there is anything inappropriate for children, by our standards (the Hays Code was fully in effect at this time, and one scene from the end of the book is omitted for this reason). It is simply that the story of the Joad family is pretty unrelievedly grim. At the end of the movie we turned to our kids and asked, "Did you know that anything like this had happened in our country?" They shook their heads solemnly.

Certainly they found the movie every bit as interesting and engaging as *Sullivan's Travels* (probably more so), running just over two hours in black and white. It is, after all, about a family and there is much one can relate to in the characters. And one can talk about the hardships of the Depression all one likes, but that doesn't quite equal the impact of watching a family's home bulldozed because they're being thrown off the land they were born on. The movie follows the Joad family as they pack up their truck and leave behind the dustbowl of Oklahoma, following a promise of fruit-picking work available in California. They stay in migrant camps, and find themselves innocently becoming strike-breakers (or "scabs"), as the farm owners exploit the influx of cheap and willing laborers. The name "Joad" echoes the long-suffering Job of the Bible, and the family endures one hardship after another largely because of Ma Joad's earthy patience and belief in family.

Jane Darwell won an Academy Award for her performance as the matriarch who holds on to the family's humanity and faith, in spite of everything. (Many of us know her from her final screen performance, as the Bird Lady in *Mary Poppins*.) Henry Fonda made full use of his persona of weary nobility as Tom Joad, the son who can never outrun the mistake of having killed a man in anger. Charley Grapewin as Grandpa had just finished playing Uncle Henry in *The Wizard of Oz* the previous year. Perhaps the strongest presence in the movie is that of director John Ford, who won the second of his record four Best Director Oscars for it. Ford tells the story in one perfect picture after another. But in spite of the visual beauty and clarity of his style, nothing ever looks posed or unnatural. Ford was a master of pictorial storytelling and drawing understated but complex performances from his actors. He is in some ways a director's director, as many great practitioners of the craft hold him up as their model.

## OCTOBER

### COMEDY/ROMANCE

# The Taming of the Shrew

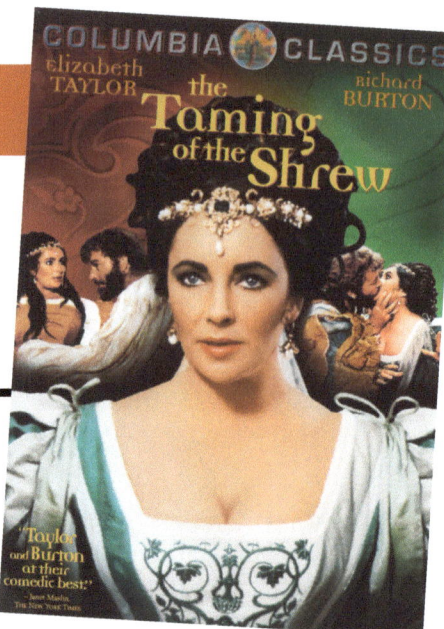

*1967, 122 minutes, color*

**Featuring Elizabeth Taylor, Richard Burton, Cyril Cusack, Michael Hordern, Michael York, Natasha Pyne, Alfred Lynch, Alan Webb, Victor Spinetti.** *Directed by Franco Zeffirelli, written by William Shakespeare*

Shakespeare's works have endured for centuries because….they're good for you. Right? Well, not exactly – and that's no way to sell them to your children. His plays were popular entertainment in their time, and that's why they survive: because they are so entertaining. Not to mention full of insight about life, fascinating characters and, by the by, brilliant language. We are lucky that Shakespeare wrote in English. And yet somehow one of the greatest writers who ever lived has been introduced to many of us as some kind of horse pill we have to swallow.

If you want to get off on the right foot in approaching the Bard, Franco Zeffirelli's *Taming of the Shrew* is an excellent place to start. It is full of great English actors who can deliver the language easily, naturally and understandably. It is directed by an Italian, who does full justice to the colorful, antic and boisterous spirit of the story, set in Padua, a medieval university town not far from Venice. And it features two megawatt movie stars, Elizabeth Taylor and Richard Burton, at the height of their beauty and charisma. (You can brush up your Shakespeare without going to the source by trying *Kiss Me, Kate*. The 1953 film of the Cole Porter musical features Howard Keel, of *Seven Brides for Seven Brothers*, playing an actor playing Petruchio opposite his real-life wife. It is full of clever pleasures, but we still urge you to sample the real thing – you will not be disappointed!)

Zeffirelli's career includes design, as well as directing for opera and film (his *Romeo and Juliet*, which came out the following year, is equally famous and equally lovely – and lively). He has a great hand with crowded Italian street scenes, such as the one that opens *The Taming of the Shrew*. Visually rich as it is, it is also the toughest scene to get your family through. This is not because it is dull or drab – quite the contrary. It is simply that so many characters, all with Italian names, are introduced very quickly – how do we know who they are? How do we tell them apart? Don't worry, it is not long before the characters and the elements of the story become very easy to recognize. There is a lovely young blonde named Bianca, and at least three men who want to be her suitors. She has an older, raven-haired sister named Katarina who is "curst" (meaning angry, rebellious and very hard to get along with). Baptista, the father of the girls, cannot give the fair Bianca in marriage until he has found a husband for the older daughter – and this promises to be no small task.

The fact that Katarina is portrayed by a luminously beautiful Elizabeth Taylor should help her chances – but, oh, that temper! There is only one man who can tame this shrew, a gentleman named Petruchio (Richard Burton) whose fortunes have waned, and who is willing to take on Kate in exchange for a generous dowry. Their wooing scene is often the occasion for a bit of slapstick in theatrical productions, but Zeffirelli turns it into a lusty romp throughout Baptista's house, ending with a jump into a huge bale of cotton that any kid would envy. This is one of the scenes that lead critics to say, approvingly, that *The Taming of the Shrew* is truly conceived as a movie, not simply a Shakespeare play on film. The physical action is always bold and funny and entirely clear. We never find ourselves scratching our heads and wondering what a character just said.

By the time Kate and Petruchio arrive at the altar, we have pretty much figured out who the various suitors are for the hand of the lovely Bianca. The one with the best chance is Lucentio, played by Michael York. (Older children, who have been allowed to see the Austin Powers movies, will recognize him as Basil Exposition, the suave head of MI5. Grownups may remember his brooding and dangerous Tybalt in Zeffirelli's *Romeo and Juliet* or his D'Artagnan in the Musketeers movies directed by Richard Lester, the Beatles' director.)  Lucentio disguises himself as a tutor, in order to spend long stretches of unsupervised time alone with Bianca.  His servant Tranio, meanwhile, has a great time impersonating his master – with inevitably comic results, when Lucentio's father arrives in town.

Possibly the greatest problem with *The Taming of the Shrew* is that contemporary audiences find the play hard to take.  Petruchio is seen as a male chauvinist fortune hunter, setting out to break the spirit of an independent woman oppressed by the customs of her time – and she even buys it, by the end, thereby becoming a traitor to the cause of women's rights!  The movie solves this problem beautifully, using nonverbal moments.  It is clear from the outset that Kate is not simply a spirited woman, she is in fact a person whose anger is expressed destructively and without any control.  The movie makes clear that violent displays of temper are not appealing in anyone, including Petruchio.  Once we see the movie's point of view that bad behavior is gender neutral, the tough treatment that Petruchio meets out to his new wife appears like harsh medicine for a serious disease.  It helps that the obvious magnetism between Taylor and Burton (who were twice married to each other off screen) makes it clear that Petruchio is attracted to more than Kate's money.  We watch him fall in love with her, so that each time he administers a tough lesson it is harder for him, and he willingly cleans his own house (literally) in order to be worthy of his new status as a married man.  The final challenge, of course, is the scene in which the couple return to Padua for Bianca's wedding feast, and the men hold a contest to see whose wife is the most obedient.  In possibly the most controversial speech Shakespeare ever wrote, we see Kate (now clearly in love with her husband as well) choosing to win the bet for him.  It is clear that Petruchio and Kate are both accomplished at play-acting to achieve their ends, that they understand each other, and that they have a long and happy union ahead of them as absolute equals.

Thus the movie brilliantly solves the central dilemma of presenting *The Taming of the Shrew* in our time.  It faced a more private challenge in our home, meeting the critical eye of the resident theater director.  With over 40 Shakespeare productions under his belt, and an apprenticeship served with an Italian master of the Commedia dell' Arte, my husband approached this film with a distinct "Show me" attitude.  To everyone's great relief, not only did the film pass muster but he became an enthusiastic convert.  The only problem was that we had to shush him as he cried out, "Michael Hordern is a

perfect Pantalone!"  The character of Baptista, the father of the girls, is indeed based on the archetypal figure of the old rich man in the Italian Commedia – and Michael Hordern is the brilliant actor who so exquisitely plays Marley's Ghost in the 1951 version of *A Christmas Carol* (or *Scrooge,* profiled in the recommended choices for December in this book).  It may or may not enrich your experience of the story to know that Petruchio is based on the figure of Capitano, the swaggering soldier who is a coward underneath.  The whole gallery of figures, the lovers, the impish servants and the tyrannical fathers, partake of the roiling spirit of the Italian comic tradition.  They were originally played with masks, but here the actors have the opportunity to accomplish a great deal nonverbally in Zeffirelli's loving close-ups.

Elizabeth Taylor, who made her reputation as a glamour goddess rather than a classical actress, absolutely holds her own here and delivers the text with clarity and confidence.  Richard Burton, who was often famous for all the wrong things, reminds us that he *did* make his reputation as a fine classical actor before becoming a Hollywood star.  Cyril Cusack, another stalwart (and father to one of the acting dynasties Britain tends to create), is delightful as Grumio, Petruchio's slovenly servant and "partner in crime."  Every performance is pitch perfect, the movie is visually gorgeous, the comedy is broad and bumptious, and the romance is heartfelt.  What better introduction to the Bard?

## OCTOBER
### HORROR/SCI-FI

# Frankenstein

*1931, 71 minutes, black-and-white*

**Featuring Colin Clive, Mae Clarke, John Boles, Boris Karloff, Edward Van Sloan, Dwight Frye.** *Directed by James Whale, written by Francis Edward Faragoh and Garrett Fort, based on the novel by Mary Shelley*

# Bride of Frankenstein

*1935, 75 minutes, black-and-white*

**Featuring Boris Karloff, Colin Clive, Valerie Hobson, Ernest Thesiger, Elsa Lanchester.** *Directed by James Whale, written by William Hurlbut and John Balderston*

As Halloween approaches, we find ourselves surrounded by images of witches and mummies and oh-so-familiar monsters. Frankenstein's monster is one that is so very familiar, it can come as a surprise to realize one hasn't actually seen the original movies that introduced the character. The 1931 *Dracula* in which Bela Lugosi gave his iconic performance as the undead Count, although relatively short (75 minutes), is rather creaky — with special effects that look campy now. It is a pleasure then to discover that the two Frankenstein movies from the same period actually hold up very well. They are suspenseful, but probably not scary enough to bother children who are already acquainted with the great lumbering figure of the monster. Besides, he never moves very fast, so one could always imagine oneself getting away.

Director James Whale was influenced by German cinematography and it is clear that he was aiming to create a strange and memorable world, not a cheap horror flick. One can look at the lighting, the angles, the moving camera in *Frankenstein*...but on a first viewing it is more fun to just give oneself over to the spookiness of the grave-robbing scene, the Gothic extravagance of Dr. Frankenstein's laboratory tower, and the perennially moody weather. One famous and delightful moment occurs when Dr. Frankenstein's assistant Fritz (precursor to the much-parodied Ygor) comes to answer a knocking at the gate. He returns up the stone stairs, but pauses for a moment to pull up his sock.

When we think of Frankenstein, we tend to think of Boris Karloff as the Monster. In fact, the name belongs to Dr. Henry Frankenstein (here played by Colin Clive), who defies the laws of nature in attempting to bring life to a creature stitched together from dead flesh, harvested from graveyards and execution sites. Mary Shelley's story invites us to recoil at Dr. Frankenstein's attempt to play God. She also refuses to reveal the exact means by which he intends to bring the creature to life, but the movie suggests that somehow electrical currents harnessed from nature are involved.

The irony is that, while we are horrified and frightened by Dr. Frankenstein's experiment, we cannot help feeling pity and perhaps affection for its misshapen result. Boris Karloff's performance is one of those in which the actor's imprint on the role is a lasting one. He created a figure that experiences human feelings, but is confused by how to act on them, and tormented by his inability to express himself. Through Fritz's error, stealing a brain from a university laboratory without reading the label, the creature is brought to life with the brain of a criminal – but also, it seems, with the heart of a child. Karloff's physicality mimics that of a toddler, with staggering steps that struggle for equilibrium. His outstretched arms help him balance (and sometimes seem to beseech), but they are misunderstood by those who think he is using them to attack.

Boris Karloff off screen loved children and was very popular with them. (His voice is never heard in the first Frankenstein film and rarely in the sequel, but we get to hear him as the narrator of the classic animated *How the Grinch Stole Christmas*.) Perhaps this connection with children explains the effectiveness of the most controversial scene of the first movie, in which the Frankenstein Monster sits by a lake with a young girl who is tossing flowers into the water. He gets the idea that the game involves throwing pretty things into the lake so, running out of flowers, he picks up the prettiest thing he sees, the girl herself, and tosses her in. Early versions of the movie censored this scene and cut directly to the image of the father carrying the body of the drowned girl toward a crowd of villagers at a festival. This actually made things worse, as the audience was left to speculate what the Monster might have done to the poor girl by the lake. Ultimately the scene was restored, making clear again the innocent mistake that leads to the tragedy, and to the Monster being feared and hunted by the people of the town.

At 71 minutes, not much longer than a primetime television show, it is entirely doable to watch *Frankenstein* and its sequel in the same evening. *Bride of Frankenstein* (75 minutes) is that rarest of Hollywood items: a sequel that is considered as good as its predecessor, if not better. It opens, in classic "it was a dark and stormy night" style, with a prologue in which Mary Shelley, who wrote the original Frankenstein story in 1818, discusses her creation with the poets Lord Byron and her husband Percy Bysshe Shelley. Elsa Lanchester (who was, in real life, married to the actor Charles Laughton) appears first as Mary Shelley and later as the Bride intended for Frankenstein's Monster. Your children may remember her as another frighteningly forbidding character, later in her career: Katie Nanna, the governess who is quitting her job at the beginning of *Mary Poppins*. It is almost the end of the film before the Bride's bandages are unwrapped. Her hissing, spitting horror at the sight of her intended husband was apparently inspired by the behavior of swans Ms. Lanchester observed in Regents Park in her native London.

Before she appears, we meet Dr. Pretorius (Ernest Thesiger), a true mad scientist and Dr. Henry Frankenstein's mentor. Colin Clive is back as Henry, playing many of his scenes seated because he had broken his leg in a horse-riding accident shortly before filming began. Boris Karloff also broke a leg, although it was on set, falling into

*At 71 minutes, it is entirely doable to watch Frankenstein and its sequel in the same evening.*

the well under the burnt windmill at the beginning of the film. Fortunately the metal struts he wore to stiffen his gait held his bones in place until they could be set. During the shoot he sweated off 20 pounds in the heavy makeup and clothing. Elsa Lanchester also suffered great physical hardships from the design of her costume and makeup. Her hair was teased up over a wire cage to create the Bride's iconic "do," she was placed on stilts that raised her 5'4" height to 7 feet, had her eyes taped open in constant horror, and was wrapped so tightly that she could not move on her own. These indignities may be forgotten, but the work of Universal Studio makeup designer Jack Pierce is immortal. (Lanchester said that he arrived on set all dressed in white, as if he were a doctor ready to perform surgery – or perhaps a Dr. Frankenstein ready to fashion a creature?)

In *Bride of Frankenstein* the Monster was required to speak, so he does not have the sunken cheeks of the first film, because Karloff could not remove his temporary bridgework as he had done before. Karloff protested the decision, as he thought the Monster's inarticulateness was what made him touching. He was too good an actor, however, to do anything but deepen the soul of the character. In one scene the Monster follows the music of a violin to the home of a hermit who, because he is blind, is not frightened of him. Here he learns the words "friend" and "good." But the Monster is never at peace for long, as fire and local townspeople terrify him. One of the most famous quotes in all of film horror history comes in the first movie, when Dr. Frankenstein beholds the stirrings of life in the creature and cries, with Colin Clive's signature edge of hysteria, "It's alive! It's alive!" And equally famous, but more affecting moment, ends the story of the Monster and his would-be Bride. Seeing that she, who was created to put an end to his loneliness, recoils from him, the Monster sends Dr. Frankenstein and his new bride Elizabeth out of the laboratory to safety. He calls upon his own Bride to stay with him while he, despairing, destroys their surroundings because "We belong dead."

Of course, not really dead, because another sequel followed (*Son of Frankenstein*, 1939) and another and another and another. And not really dead because, when all is said and done, you can't keep a good monster down.

## OCTOBER

### COMEDY/HORROR

# Abbott and Costello Meet Frankenstein

(also shown as **Bud Abbott Lou Costello Meet Frankenstein**)

*1948, 83 minutes, black-and-white*

**Featuring Bud Abbott, Lou Costello, Lon Chaney, Jr., Bela Lugosi, Glenn Strange.** *Directed by Charles Barton, written by Robert Lees, Frederic I. Rinaldo and John Grant*

Anyone who has ever enjoyed the classic version of "Who's On First?" has been introduced to the comedy team of Bud Abbott and Lou Costello. Abbott and Costello emerged from vaudeville and then radio, to become hugely successful movie stars during the Second World War. Tall, lean Bud Abbott served as straight man to short, chubby comic bumbler Lou Costello. Contrast is the key to successful comedy duos (think Laurel and Hardy, George Burns and Gracie Allen, …). When the pair's fast-talking east coast voices were deemed to hard to tell apart on radio, Costello adopted a higher-pitched voice for contrast. Before long they, and their routines, were everywhere.

With *Abbott and Costello Meet Frankenstein*, the pair initiated a series of successful meetings (they went on to meet the Mummy, the Invisible Man, Dr. Jekyll and Mr. Hyde, the Keystone Kops and more). This first one is packed with three of the great movie monsters: Frankenstein, Dracula and the Wolf Man. And, as a bonus, Dracula is played by Bela Lugosi (who created the role in the original film) and the Wolf Man by Lon Chaney, Jr. (the original Wolf Man). Boris Karloff, who originated the role of Frankenstein's monster, declined to appear and the role went instead to Glenn Strange, who had inherited it from Karloff in several films after the 1931 original. *Abbott and Costello Meet Frankenstein* would make a great movie to watch after trick or treating on Halloween night – not only because of the bumper crop of monsters it features, but because once the potential scariness of the evening has devolved into a series of bumblebees and fairy princesses at the front door, it seems only fitting to relax with a movie in which the chills and the laughs are fairly evenly balanced. And you are offering the family the best of Bud Abbott and Lou Costello while you're at it.

In this movie, you won't hear Costello's signature "Heyyyyy, Abbott!" Abbott goes by the character name of Chick Young here, and he plays a baggage handler in a small Florida town. When Costello, as his partner Wilbur Grey, mishandles some large incoming crates, they are obliged to deliver them personally to 'MacDougal's House of Horrors' for insurance inspection. They are told these are museum exhibits: the remains of Dracula and the body of the Frankenstein monster. They are, in fact, the beginnings of a plot concocted by Dracula to implant Wilbur's brain in the head of the Frankenstein monster. Why not? Add in Larry Talbot, or the Wolf Man, who has tracked these 'exhibits' from Europe and is determined to stop the plot. Lon Chaney's Wolf Man (very like the ex-convict he played in *The Defiant Ones*) is basically a decent man who's gone through some pretty rough times. The fun comes in watching him transform from good guy to scary guy when the full moon rises. The whole arsenal of horror film devices is put to comic effect: revolving walls, underground passageways, creepy laboratories, costume balls…and, of course, Lou Costello barely able to speak when he is frightened. Bud Abbott's straight man is sometimes more cranky than simply straight. Still, when the pair finally encounter, at the very end of the film, a cigarette suspended in midair and the voice of Vincent Price introducing himself as the Invisible Man, we know they are on to something…

# NOVEMBER

### DRAMA

# Mr. Smith Goes to Washington

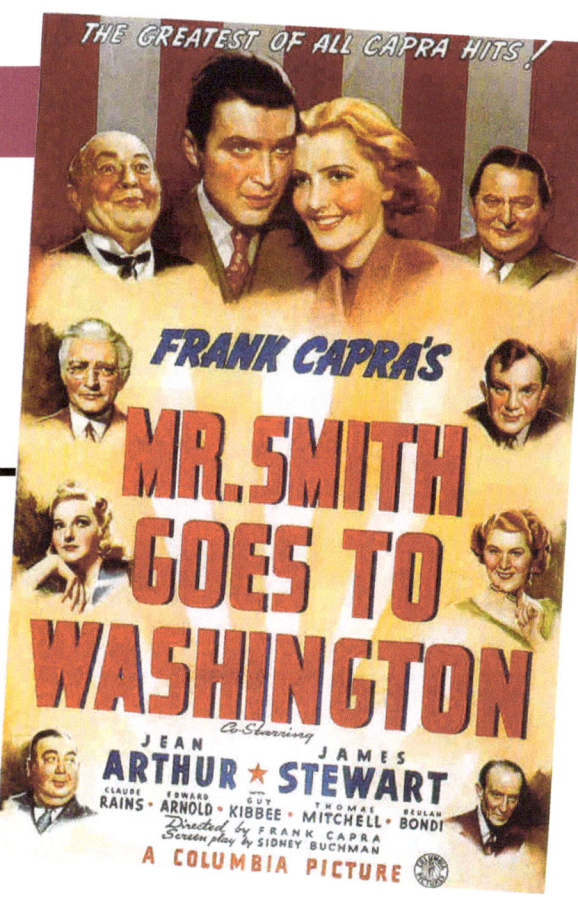

*1939, 129 minutes, black-and-white*

**Featuring Jean Arthur, James Stewart, Claude Rains, Edward Arnold, Thomas Mitchell, Harry Carey.** *Directed by Frank Capra, written by Sidney Buchman*

The first Tuesday in November is Election Day in the United States. Not every year offers an historic opportunity to elect a new president. But every year does offer an opportunity to engage the family in the important issues faced by citizens in a democracy. *Mr. Smith Goes to Washington* tells the story of Jefferson Smith, a man who, in an unlikely turn of fate, is suddenly plucked from obscurity and sent to Washington as a U.S. Senator. There his innocent belief in the power of government to do well comes face to face with the cynical corruption of many of the players in the government game.

This was James Stewart's breakout role, in a year which also brought to the screen *The Wizard of Oz* and *Gone with the Wind*. Jefferson Smith is a young everyman from a town out west (possibly Montana), appointed to a Senate seat suddenly left vacant by the death of the sitting Senator. The role fit Stewart beautifully, making the most of his inherent decency and aw-shucks form of self-deprecation. Smith is involved with a group of kids called the Boy Rangers in the movie (just as Stewart was personally involved with the Boy Scouts in private life). The governor of his state, who is in cahoots with a corrupt and powerful newspaper owner named Jim Taylor, appoints Smith to the Senate seat in the belief that his youth and inexperience will make him easy to manipulate. This turns out to be quite a miscalculation on the governor's part: he does not factor in a Boy Ranger's inalienable desire to do good.

The opening scenes of the movie can be a bit hard to follow unless one is familiar with some of the peculiarities of American politics. Each state sends a junior and a senior senator to the national Senate. When a U.S. Senator dies in office, or is unable to complete his or her term, the Governor of that Senator's state appoints someone to finish the term. This is perhaps the only way someone can wind up in the position of U.S. Senator without having run for election. As the film begins, we see the boys in the back room back home having a field day trying to influence the Governor's choice – until he pretty much makes his decision based on the flip of a coin.

As the new junior senator for his state, Mr. Jefferson Smith goes to Washington to join the senior senator, Joseph Paine, who has held office for many years and was a close friend of Smith's late father. As Senator Paine, the suave Claude Rains makes a strong bid to steal the film (and this is three years before he almost walked off with *Casablanca*, as the cheerful opportunist Captain Renault). Paine is bemused by the younger man's wide-eyed idealism, something he has long since lost in the gritty, real world of backroom politics. Yet one senses that he misses his own ideals, and the heart of the story has much to do with whether witnessing Smith's commitment to them can help him reclaim his own integrity.

Mr. Smith has that effect on people. Another world-weary cynic he wins over is his aide Clarissa Saunders, a veteran of the halls of power played by Jean Arthur. (With her distinctive, emotionally rich voice and the core of

*Every year does offer an opportunity to engage the family in the important issues faced by citizens in a democracy.*

vulnerability under her strong exterior, Arthur was later summoned out of retirement to play the rancher's wife in *Shane*.) Jefferson Smith has been encouraged to present a bill in the Senate, mainly to keep him occupied and out of mischief. As it turns out, his proposal to establish a camp for the Boy Rangers on an idyllic lakeside in his home state runs straight up against the dam-building and profiteering plans of the cabal who sent him to Washington.

It is Saunders who decides that Smith is worthy of rescue in this tough world, and coaches him in the art of the filibuster: a last-stand tactic designed to tie up the forward movement of a bill. This will also take a little explaining, in order to fully enjoy the drama of Mr. Smith's accomplishment. As long as a Senator can hold the Senate floor and keep talking – all night, if need be – he or she can prevent a bill from being put to a vote and effectively put to bed. While Smith keeps talking, to try to prevent the dam from being approved and himself from being expelled from the Senate, Jim Taylor (the corrupt newspaperman back home) is doing everything in his power to demolish Smith's reputation and hopes.

When *Mr. Smith Goes to Washington* was first released, it was not warmly welcomed by members of the U.S. Senate, who objected to the unflattering portrait of their august body. They did not enjoy the undignified idea of the President of the Senate (played by the ever-paternal, all-American character actor Harry Carey) winking at an attractive young woman in the visitors' gallery to encourage a filibuster. Nor were they pleased at the picture of corruption in high office, and political muscle being used in the streets, to the point of Boy Rangers being roughed up and honest citizens' efforts suppressed. It is useful to remember, though, that although Frank Capra may have been at pains to make this movie look realistic (even having the Senate chamber studied and then carefully reproduced as a set), fantasy is often an important element in his films. Think of his 1946 venture with

James Stewart, *It's a Wonderful Life*. It features beautifully recognizable scenes of small-town American life, but in which the story is framed and underpinned by events at least as fantastical as the tale of hayseed-becomes-a-Senator.

Many film critics look askance at Frank Capra, as having a sentimental and gauzy view of America. That makes it especially important to remember that *Mr. Smith Goes to Washington* carried quite a sting when it first appeared. Joseph Kennedy, the ambassador to Great Britain, was afraid it would tarnish America's reputation abroad, and it was banned in a number of totalitarian countries, where the idea of an honest individual standing up to entrenched governmental corruption was not welcome. It may be that Mr. Capra, like Mr. Smith, has gradually won us over with his idealism (since now the movie is regarded as a classic, and a great statement of American political values). In the shots which show Jefferson Smith visiting the great monuments of the nation's capital, we are invited to choose with whom we would rather side: the cynical power-brokers who consider him a bumpkin, or the young man who is naïve enough to be awed and moved by the great principles these monuments represent. We are asked to imagine that an unlikely individual, believing in those principles, could make it to Washington – and make a difference. This is a great movie to show your children when you are telling them "Yes, you can."

# NOVEMBER

## ADVNTURE/DRAMA/ROMANCE

# The African Queen

*1951, 105 minutes, color*

**Featuring Humphrey Bogart, Katharine Hepburn, Robert Morley, Peter Bull, Theodore Bikel.** *Directed by John Huston, adapted by James Agee, John Huston and Peter Viertel*

A road movie, or a buddy movie, sends a couple of characters on an adventure together, and gives us the double pleasure of watching the adventure and watching how it changes the characters. If the pair happen to be a man and a woman, you get the added dimension of unfolding romance. If the actors happen to be superstars, you get *It Happened One Night*…or *The African Queen*.

Humphrey Bogart and Katharine Hepburn were at the height of their careers when they agreed to travel to Africa with legendary director John Huston to shoot this film. Bogart plays Charlie Allnut, the hard-drinking captain of the riverboat the African Queen. Hepburn is Rose Sayer, a spinster who has spent 10 years supporting her brother's missionary efforts in a village in the Belgian Congo. Charlie Allnut brings mail and supplies to the mission, and as the story begins he brings news of the beginning of the First World War. The African setting makes it hard to imagine the story was set so long ago – it feels relatively contemporary. But German soldiers soon appear, set fire to the village and chase away the natives, and beat Rose's brother, played by British actor Robert Morley. The Reverend Sayer lapses into delirium. In his feverish babblings we learn that he would much rather be comfortably at home in England but has failed into the missionary service, and decided to take his sister Rose along as she is "not comely among the maidens."

The Reverend's death leaves Rose entirely abandoned, sitting alone on the deck of their home waiting for whatever fate might await her. That fate turns out to be the return of Charlie Allnut, who is obliged to take her along with him on the African Queen. Katharine Hepburn plays to all her strengths here, as superstars are often expected to do. Her straight-backed Connecticut upbringing serves the straitlaced missionary's sister well – but we know that in her heart she will be up for an adventure, and ready to be an equal partner with any man. Bogart, for his part, is familiar in the role of a worldly cynic who cannot resist his own tender heart and essentially noble character.

At the end of their river is a lake patrolled by a German gunboat, the Louisa. Charlie claims that its presence prevents any possibility of a British military presence in their area. But Rose departs from her pacifist missionary ways and devises a plan to turn the African Queen into a torpedo boat, to sink the Louisa. It is a bold and unexpected idea, and it is her determination (and the sacrifice of many bottles of Gordon's gin) that allows them to get through several sets of rapids, plenty of company from the wildlife, and all of Charlie Allnut's doubts. It is a great treat to watch these two pros play together, and trace the gradual evolution from "Mr. Allnut" and "Miss" to "dear" and "Rosie."

We spend most of the movie in the company of these two marvelous actors. But the film is not really a two-hander. There is a third character almost always present: the African Queen herself. She has plenty of personality, having worked as a steam boat for 40 years before this starring role. She is the 'engine' of the plot, the location for the romance and, ultimately, acts almost as an independent agent in the sinking of the Louisa. (By this time, Charlie Allnut has transferred his bachelor loyalty to his boat, and now has a new love – perhaps it is Rose Sayer who, in the end, becomes the "African Queen.") The boat itself was too small to accommodate camera and crew for many of the more intimate scenes, so parts of the boat

were reconstructed on a raft that allowed space for filming. It is a model of the boat that we see shooting the most dangerous set of rapids. The African Queen went on to perform again in *White Hunter, Black Heart*, a 1990 Clint Eastwood film based on a book by Peter Viertel, an uncredited contributor to the screenplay of *The African Queen*. It tells the story of a film director in Africa, obsessed with hunting – clearly based on John Huston, on location for this movie.

Filming on location was relatively unusual, and thoroughly adventurous at the time, and the shoot itself engendered plenty of stories. Hepburn wrote a book about it entitled "The Making of *The African Queen*: How I Went to Africa with Bogart, Bacall and Huston and Almost Lost My Mind." Lauren Bacall was there acting as den mother for her husband and the production team, although it is unlikely that even her presence added much glamour to the surroundings. Various forms of water- and insect-borne illness ran rampant through the entire production much of the time. Apparently Bogart and Huston were spared because they drank so much Scotch that any insect with the temerity to bite one of them met its own quick fate.

Bogart came out of *The African Queen* with one souvenir: the only Best Actor Oscar of his career. Although

> *Filming on location was relatively unusual, and thoroughly adventurous at the time, and the shoot itself engendered plenty of stories.*

we can't help continuing to note the winners, the Academy Awards are a bit of a roulette wheel, at best. Sometimes well-deserving performances are overlooked and then, a few years later, the Academy seems to be trying to make up for its oversight by presenting the Oscar for an offbeat role by the same actor, or a kind of lifetime achievement award for a performance that didn't cause the actor to break much of a sweat. Some actors wind up being overlooked entirely – like Cary Grant, whose fatal mistake was to make it all look so easy. In the case of Bogart's win, one can't help feeling the Academy was tickled to see the famously cool star allow himself to play a scene in which his rumbling stomach provides teatime awkwardness for the missionary and his proper sister. Katharine Hepburn was nominated for Best Actress for Rose Sayer, but didn't win. That does not diminish her stature as the actress most recognized by the Academy: with four Oscars out of twelve nominations. The African Queen herself was not eligible for nomination, but went on to inspire the "Jungle Cruise" attraction at Disneyland. She is now comfortably retired and can be visited in Key Largo (a place closely associated with another famous Bogart/John Huston film). There the Queen was finally recognized when she joined, in 1992, the U.S. National Register of Historic Places.

# NOVEMBER

## THRILLER/ROMANCE/COMEDY

# To Catch a Thief

*1955, 106 minutes, color*

**Featuring Cary Grant, Grace Kelly, Jessie Royce Landis, John Williams, Charles Vanel, Brigitte Auber.** *Directed by Alfred Hitchcock, screenplay by John Michael Hayes*

"Good evening…" Meet Alfred Hitchcock, the Master of Suspense. Over a career of many decades, Mr. Hitchcock directed many masterpieces, some near-misses and a few clunkers. He also virtually created (for Americans) the notion of the director as star. By the time his television series, *Alfred Hitchcock Presents*, began airing in 1955, he had a sterling reputation as a director of thrillers, and some of his most famous work still ahead of him. He was always ready to exploit his own persona: bald, rotund, with a quietly droll English fascination with all things macabre and murderous. At the opening of each episode, viewers would see his caricature in profile, then the man himself turning to the camera and drily intoning, "Good evening…"

Hitchcock also slipped a cameo appearance into all his feature films. The signature moment would usually occur early in the movie, so the audience could then relax their vigilance and just get into the story. Possibly the ultimate must-see Hitchcock film is *Psycho* (1963), but it is not – seriously *not* a family film. This is a concern with several of his movies, and yet one needs to be aware of the The Master. (Our family enjoyed a screening of *Rear Window*, reveling in James Stewart's performance, the fascinating tapestry of humanity he views through his window, the almost complete lack of overt violence. And then, much as I hated to dampen everyone's enthusiasm, I felt obliged to ask, "But didn't Raymond Burr's character actually, um, *dismember* his wife's body?" Well, yes… he did.)

The trick is to land somewhere between Hitch's earliest outings, made in England in black and white (in spite of their great virtues, the children may regard them as quaint) and some of his later movies, made after years in America. These can be very grown-up (like *Vertigo*) or real contenders for producing nightmares (like *The Birds*). Between the Scylla and Charybdis of creaky and terrifying, we find *To Catch a Thief*. It offers Cary Grant, Grace Kelly, a light touch and a travelogue setting on the French Riviera.

Grant plays John Robie, a retired cat burglar who now lives quietly in a magnificent villa overlooking the Mediterranean. Several shots of cats in the opening sequence tempt us to believe that perhaps Robie is still active as the Cat, prowling the rooftops of luxury hotels to steal rich women's jewelry. The Cat was stopped in his career by a stint in prison, but now someone is at it again. The police arrive to arrest Robie on suspicion, but he evades them like a cat – and makes a leisurely escape on a local bus, seated next to Alfred Hitchcock (in the director's famous cameo). He seeks out his old buddies from the French Resistance, which he joined after sharing a jail cell with them. His friend Bertani has staffed the kitchen of his restaurant almost entirely with the old gang. They are angry because Robie continues to live free, while they are all on probation – and an active cat burglar could scare away the wealthy tourists on whom their livelihood depends, or discredit the good behavior on which their parole depends. Robie decides that the only way to clear his name is to catch a thief – and prove that it is not him! This he sets out to do with the help of an insurance agent, H.H. Hughson (John Williams, whom we have seen as Sabrina's father, and as the lawyer who almost defends Vole in *Witness for the Prosecution*).

*In one film after another, Alfred Hitchcock explored his fascination with cool, beautiful blondes – and Grace Kelly was perhaps his favorite embodiment of this archetype.*

Cary Grant was coaxed out of an 18-month retirement to make this movie. With the ascendance of Marlon Brando and the Actors Studio style of acting, Grant felt his era had passed: the time of the debonair leading man, equally gifted at repartee, romance and wearing a tailored suit. Fortunately, Grant could not resist the chance to work again with Hitchcock (who called him "the only actor I ever loved"). The movie was a great hit, and Grant went on acting for another 11 years. Watching Cary Grant move with lithe and feline grace, one can see why he was an inspiration for Ian Fleming's character of James Bond, as well as a top contender for the role. When *Dr. No* was filmed, Grant was considered too old at 58 – and considering what a long-running franchise it has become, it may be just as well. In *To Catch a Thief* he is a mere 50, and in peak condition.

Throughout his career, Grant did many of his own stunts and displayed a physical confidence that was firmly rooted in his earliest experiences on stage. Starting life as a neglected English boy, Archibald Leach dropped out of school at 14 and became stilt-walker for a traveling troupe that specialized in acrobatics and knockabout comedy. His greatest role, perhaps, was Cary Grant (the name he adopted and the persona he created). When told that everyone wanted to be Cary Grant, his answer was "So do I." In roles from *Bringing Up Baby* and *Philadelphia Story* to Hitchcock's *Notorious*, we see his extraordinary precision, timing and charm, and also great versatility and depth. Strangely, the Oscar for Best Actor eluded him throughout his career. This may have been partly because he was one of the first actors whose celebrity allowed him to escape the studio system and gain control of his own career (the Academy finally did honor him with a Lifetime Achievement Award in 1970). It is also, no doubt, because he excelled at the hardest acting job of all: he made it look effortless.

In one film after another, Alfred Hitchcock explored his fascination with cool, beautiful blondes – and Grace Kelly was perhaps his favorite embodiment of this archetype. *To Catch a Thief* was the third and last of their collaborations (after *Dial M for Murder* and *Rear Window*). A few years later Hitch offered her the lead in *Marnie*, but she was engaged in another long-running role which prevented her from accepting: that of Princess Grace of Monaco. There is some poignancy to the shots of Kelly driving her sports car along a spectacular mountain road in *To Catch a Thief*, as this was the setting where she met her untimely death in 1982.

It is probably best not to dwell on that kind of thought, but rather to enjoy the delicious chemistry she had with Cary Grant and some of the sly innuendo they were able to slip into the script. One can savor the rather unlikely prospect of Grant trying to gain the confidence of a wealthy widow (Jessie Royce Landis, playing Kelly's mother) by passing himself off as a lumber baron from Oregon State, and wondering if he would be more credible if he called out "Timber!" from time to time. On the less wry side, one finds the spectacular costumes fashioned by the legendary designer Edith Head for the masquerade ball sequence. Or the fireworks that light up the sky outside the hotel window, as Grant and Kelly recline on the couch together. The display goes on and on – and on, until one has to wonder whether Hitchcock is winking at us rather unsubtly. Or whether, perhaps, sometimes fireworks are only fireworks...

# NOVEMBER

## MUSICAL/COMEDY/ROMANCE

# Top Hat

*1935, 81 minutes, black-and-white*

**Featuring Fred Astaire, Ginger Rogers, Edward Everett Horton, Erik Rhodes, Eric Blore, Helen Broderick.** *Directed by Mark Sandrich, written by Dwight Taylor and Allan Scott*

Peanut butter and jelly. Champagne and bubbles. Fred and Ginger. Some things will always go together. Fred Astaire danced with many partners in many movies – but the gold standard remains Fred Astaire and Ginger Rogers. Fred was always debonair, romantic and a sublime dance partner. Some wags like to point out that Ginger could do everything Fred could do - backwards, wearing a skirt and high heels – but really it was her skill as an actress that lifted the partnership to legendary heights. She matched Astaire in presence or, as Katharine Hepburn apparently said, "He gives her class and she gives him sex." It's true that Astaire was light and romantic rather than powerfully masculine, but Rogers makes one feel that, however she might resist, there is no more perfect man in the world to fall in love with. Together they made ten pictures, and any one of them is bound to make you smile, no matter how dark and dreary the day may be outside. In fact, you may start hoping for the kind of day that keep you indoors watching old movies. As the lyrics in their first dance number of this one say, "Isn't it a lovely day to be caught in the rain?"

*Top Hat* is the first movie that was written expressly for Fred and Ginger – and the beginning of Astaire's collaboration with the legendary songwriter Irving Berlin. There is a popular story, concerning Fred Astaire's first screen test with RKO, that he was judged to be not a great actor, not a great singer, balding…but could dance a little. This 'non-singer' introduced (and artistically owned) many of the greatest classics of the American Songbook. He slipped them into his movies the way he slipped in the dances: easily, naturally and organically. In this movie we get our first chance to hear songs now familiar and well loved, like "Cheek to Cheek," "Isn't It a Lovely Day" and the song from which the movie takes its name, "Top Hat, White Tie and Tails."

This last number does not slip unobtrusively into the action: it is a big production number featuring Jerry Travers, Astaire's character, an American entertainer. Nowhere will you see a better version of the number in which Manhattanites in formal dress are out on the town. It culminates in a brilliantly inventive sequence in which Astaire dispatches one chorus member after another, with his cane standing in for various kinds of weaponry and his tap shoes providing the sharp crack of artillery. The complexity of the number required that it be shot in several takes, which was unusual for Astaire. After rehearsing obsessively to ensure every move was perfect, he liked to film dances in one take with the camera in a fixed position. This was in contrast to the Busby Berkeley style of dance staging, with swooping crane shots and aerial views of the chorus kicking their legs in patterns like a living kaleidoscope. Astaire believed that the dancers' entire bodies should be seen within a fixed frame (like the proscenium of a stage). The variety of rhythms and steps were where the drama and artistry lay: "Either the camera dances, or I will."

Jerry Travers is in London to do a show (we open with a delightful scene of him tapping some life into a startled group at a stuffy, exclusive men's club). His producer,

Horace Hardwicke, is played by Edward Everett Horton, a master practitioner of the art of the double take. Hardwicke's lock-jawed English valet Bates is played by Eric Blore, a stalwart in no fewer than five Astaire-Rogers films. The feud between man and manservant over the correct shape of a tie is sheer comic delight. It is in Hardwicke's hotel suite that Jerry meets fashion model Dale Tremont (Ginger Rogers) and falls for her. The "affliction" that causes him to burst spontaneously into tap routines has awakened her. Jerry's charm offensive begins when Dale returns to her room downstairs. He spreads sand on the floor, from the ashtray standing in the hall, and performs a tender soft-shoe (affectionately quoted by later dancers) in an attempt to act as Dale's personal sandman. He is soon having flowers delivered to Dale's room from the hotel florist shop, where one can briefly spot a young Lucille Ball playing a clerk.

Although the film relies on an ensemble of six performers, it sets out to weave the most complex dilemmas possible. Horace's wife Madge wants to introduce Jerry to a certain someone, and the men have to fly to Venice for the weekend to accommodate her plan. While Horace's wandering eye is a familiar feature of the middle-aged husband, Madge is anything but the battle-axe one might expect to have reining him in. Delightfully played by Helen Broderick, she has been there, done that and knows how to manage her man. The tangle of mistaken identities that fuels the plot is drawn out much longer than is credible. But, hey, that candy-cane recreation of a Venetian canal doesn't look too credible either – this is a musical, remember? And the plot can't resolve until Astaire and Rogers have had the chance to dance cheek to cheek, guilty, confused and now irresistibly in love. We wait in vain, though, to witness the moment when the farcical mix-up is explained to the lovers. About ten minutes were cut from the last part of the movie after early previews because of concerns about length: perhaps that scene hit the cutting room floor.

Adding further comic complication is Erik Rhodes as Alberto Beddini, who designs the clothes Dale is modeling and who provides a satirical over-the-top version of a jealous Italian lover. One gown that Beddini might not wish to take credit for is the feathered creation Ginger wears in "Cheek to Cheek" (and which the actress herself chose and insisted upon). The dress shed so much that Astaire claimed it was "like a chicken attacked by a

*Fred Astaire and Ginger Rogers with Irving Berlin at the piano*

coyote." Once the feathers were more securely stitched on, and Astaire recovered from his frustration, the incident won Rogers the nickname "Feathers" and a teasing reference in a dance number in *Easter Parade*. Rogers was not alone in having some say over her wardrobe. The ever-dapper Astaire had a lasting influence on men's clothing styles with his own personal look of tailored sport jackets and easy-cut slacks, giving him freedom of movement and an elegant nonchalance.

Dance aficionados often cite *Swing Time* (1936) as their favorite Astaire-Rogers pairing, because of the exceptional variety and quality of the dances it features. It is, indeed, a wonderful movie, every bit as funny and romantic as *Top Hat* and full of favorite songs by Jerome Kern and Dorothy Fields: "Pick Yourself Up (Dust yourself off)," "The Way You Look Tonight," "A Fine Romance" and "Never Gonna Dance," to name a few. It also contains one scene with a major Tricky Bit. In a tribute to Bill "Bojangles" Robinson, Astaire performs in black-face on a set which features giant feet opening to reveal long legs and a caricature African-American face. Astaire's admiration for Robinson was profound, but here it is expressed in the idiom of the '30s, which requires navigating some awkward shoals for a contemporary audience. It is worth it because Astaire's spirit is always imbued with respect: for his partner, for the dance, for the audience. Respect, discipline and high-spirited fun…if you are watching one of these movies around the Thanksgiving holiday, be sure to give thanks for the way that Fred Astaire embodied these values, and for the wonderful evenings we get to spend with him, again and again.

# NOVEMBER

### ADVENTURE/BIOGRAPHY/DRAMA

## Lawrence of Arabia

*1962, 216 minutes, color*

**Featuring Peter O'Toole, Alec Guinness, Anthony Quinn, Jack Hawkins, Omar Sharif, Jose Ferrer, Anthony Quayle, Claude Rains.** *Directed by David Lean, written by Robert Bolt and Michael Wilson*

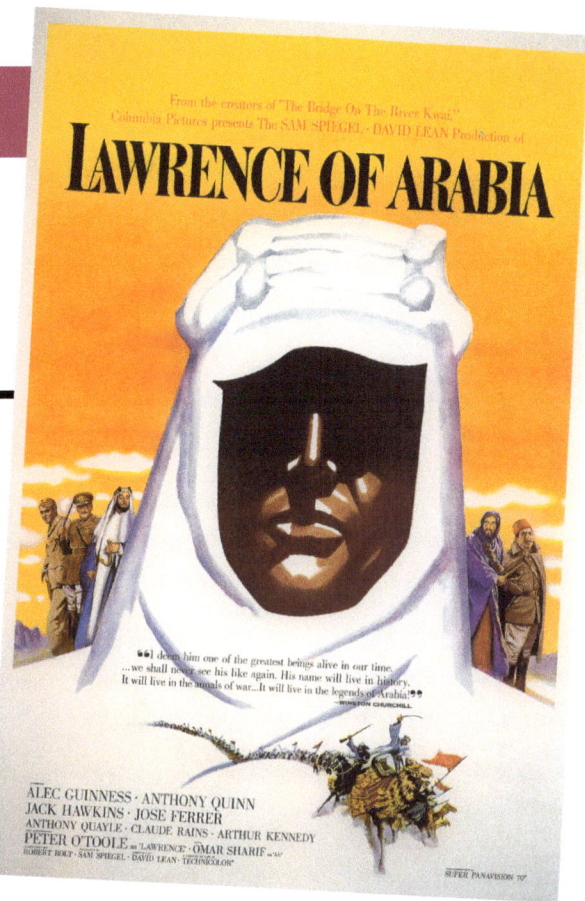

Are you ready for a big fat movie? *Lawrence of Arabia* is nothing if not a Big Fat Movie – epic in its scope, its ambitions and its stature in modern film. Like *My Fair Lady*, it hails from a time when a major release could run over 3 hours – complete with musical overture and intermission – but would pack an astonishing amount of cinematic pleasure in every frame. With its bright, hot Middle Eastern settings, it is a terrific world to visit on a dreary November evening. The word used to be that subliminal messages like "Buy Coca-Cola" were flashed on the screen during movie intermissions. But the Oscar-winning cinematography in *Lawrence of Arabia* so beautifully evokes the desert scenes that you will hardly need any prompting. Be sure to keep some cold drinks nearby, and maybe a fan.

British director David Lean completed *The Bridge on the River Kwai* before taking on the story of T.E. Lawrence, and he followed it up with *Doctor Zhivago* – a very impressive trio of films in an over-all impressive career. Like many great directors, Lean tended to develop almost his own company of actors, with whom he worked repeatedly (this was true of Preston Sturges, Alfred Hitchcock, Elia Kazan and, of course, the great foreign directors Ingmar Bergman, Federico Fellini and Akira Kurosawa). The cast of *Lawrence of Arabia* is so exceptionally strong that one is obliged to forgive the story for offering not one single speaking role for a woman. It is an adventure tale, definitely not a romance. Well, not a conventional romance. The story traces the growing passion of an Englishman, T.E. Lawrence for the unforgiving beauty of the desert, for the tribal people he meets there and for the cause of freedom they take up against the rule of the Ottoman Empire.

When we think of World War I, we tend to think of muddy trenches in France, and forget that one of Germany's major allies was the Ottoman Empire ruled from what is now Turkey. And that one of the major events of the First World War was the Arab Revolt, 1916-1918, in which Britain and France encouraged local Arab tribes to rise up against their Ottoman rulers, with the promise of their own independence as a goal. T.E. Lawrence was working in the Middle East as an archeologist when he joined the British Army, and his knowledge of Arabic and of local geography proved to be strategically valuable to his commanders. He was sent to assess the prospects for Prince Feisal to succeed in a revolt, and found himself becoming first a respected adviser to the prince and, before long, a leader in uniting the various tribes in common cause against the Turks.

The story plays out on a large historical canvas, but the movie has more the feel of a western than an epic. This is because David Lean had Robert Bolt rewrite the original script in order to focus closely on the character of Lawrence. Many of the elements of a classic western are here: the cool stranger who rides in from a mysterious past, proves himself through feats of courage and endurance, gradually gains the trust of the local folk, changes the way he dresses as a mark of acceptance, is enlisted to help his new friends in a conflict, leads them in a fight against the bad guys in spite of overwhelming

> *The story plays out on a large historical canvas, but the movie has more the feel of a western than an epic.*

odds, suffers inner torment about the use of violence, then finally has to move on because his job is done and the community needs to find its way without him. (Does this sound familiar? Alan Ladd, the star of *Shane*, desperately wanted the part of Lawrence in this movie, but David Lean went with O'Toole instead.) Lawrence became a legend in much the way a lone gunslinger does: by living out his singular destiny under a beating sun. Lean was a fan of John Ford's *The Searchers*, and quotes one of his images in the unforgettably long and dramatic entrance of Sherif Ali, coming directly toward the camera from a great distance through waves of heat to the desert well. Almeria in Spain, where a number of scenes were shot, became a favorite location for the later "spaghetti Westerns" of Sergio Leone.

Under the tender love story of a man and his horse (or in this case a man and his camel) lies a quintessentially British story: the adventurer who is more at home in some exotic outpost of the empire than back on England's green and pleasant shores. As an illegitimate child, Lawrence was bound to find more scope for his imagination and ambitions outside the narrow confines of English society. When asked why he likes the desert, the screenplay has Lawrence answer "Because it's clean." Cleaner, no doubt, than the complications that might govern his life at home but, as Prince Feisal makes clear, this is the kind of answer only a "desert-loving Englishman" could make. The Bedouins adapted to the harsh conditions of desert life because that is where they lived, not because they had any romantic notions of natural beauty or building character. To recall Noel Coward's famous line, it is only mad dogs and Englishmen who go out in the midday sun. The desert was the one place open enough, and challenging enough, to allow T.E. Lawrence to undergo the transformation into Lawrence of Arabia.

Only in the opening of the film do we see Lawrence in the verdant countryside of Dorset, to which he retired after his long military career. We see him speeding along a country road on a motorcycle moments before his fatal accident, then meet some of the characters from his life following his funeral – and from then on the story unfolds in flashback. (If you are horrified at the sight of Lawrence riding without a helmet, you are not alone. The neurosurgeon who attended the actual Lawrence after the accident, Sir Hugh Cairns, was deeply affected and his subsequent research led to the widespread use of helmets not only in the military but for civilians.) Once we take up Lawrence's story in 1916, David Lean has the action always moving from left to right on the screen, to give the feeling of an ongoing journey. It is also notable that the scenes in Cairo which introduce the British military brass are shot in medium to long shots, which gives us a feeling of distance and lack of engagement with the action. It is only once Lawrence embarks on his adventure in the desert that Lean starts to use more close-ups, allowing us a more intimate feeling of connection to the story.

Remember, too, that none of the effects in the movie are achieved digitally. Those are actual camels creating actual hoof prints in the sand, and if the production team didn't manage to get the shot…well, the hoof prints would still be there on the second take. No, that's not a young Skywalker riding a tall hoofed creature through the deserts of the planet Tatooine, and the Alec Guinness you see in a long robe is not Obi-Wan Kenobi. But, yes, Steven Spielberg and George Lucas were both profoundly influenced by David Lean's work in this film. *Lord of the Rings* features spectacular (and digitally enhanced) scenes of horsemen sweeping across the plain, but nothing more dramatic than the daring and unexpected attack Lawrence launches on the port of Aqaba from the forbidding (and hence undefended) direction of the Nefud Desert. During the filming of this scene, Peter O'Toole once fell off his camel. Only the fact that the creature stood over him protected the actor from being trampled to death by the extras' horses.

*Lawrence of Arabia* swept the Oscars with seven awards, including Best Picture and Best Director, and Best Score for Maurice Jarre's haunting and unforgettable

music. Peter O'Toole was nominated for Best Actor but did not win, although his performance as the enigmatic and contradictory Lawrence is widely considered one of the finest on screen. Omar Sharif was also nominated (but did not win) for Best Supporting Actor for the role of Sherif Ali, who is initially skeptical of Lawrence but ultimately becomes a close ally. Already a star in the Middle East, Sharif went on to play Dr. Zhivago in David Lean's next historical epic. Included in the roundup of usual suspects in this uniformly fine cast are, of course, Alec Guinness as Prince Feisal, Claude Rains (Captain Renault in *Casablanca*) as Mr. Dryden, the diplomat who heads the Arab Bureau, and Jack Hawkins (familiar from *The Bridge on the River Kwai*) as General Allenby.

Two faces are also familiar from *The Guns of Navarone*. One is Anthony Quayle as Colonel Harry Brighton, Lawrence's immediate superior – you may recall him as the major who injured his leg and was left with the Germans in *Navarone*. The other is Anthony Quinn, who for many years served as Hollywood's all-purpose ethnic actor. Of Mexcian and Irish ancestry, he played the Greek resistance fighter Stavros in Navarone (not to mention another notable Greek named Zorba), an Italian circus performer in *La Strada*, as well as Asians, Native Americans and Inuit, Russian, Hawaiian, Filipino – even a Mexican (brother of Zapata, played by Marlon Brando, in Elia Kazan's *Viva Zapata!*) Here he is the larger than life Auda abu Tayi, leader of the Howeitat tribe. Auda is dismayed to find that the "gold" Lawrence promised in the siege of Aqaba is actually paper money. But Quinn plays him with a quality we have come to associate with him: a worldly innocence combined with the heart of a lion. He is one of the few American actors in the cast. In a brilliant stroke of 'naturalization,' the American Film Institute declared *Lawrence of Arabia* one of the top ten American movies ever made – in spite of it being an entirely British-made film. The Arab states may have gained their independence, but Hollywood's colonizing spirit is still alive and well.

**TRICKY BIT:**

Lawrence is captured by the Turks and interviewed by an officer, played rather lasciviously by Jose Ferrer. The camera cuts away before things go too far, and we eventually see Lawrence tossed out into the alley by a Turkish soldier. At which point my kids asked me, "What happened?" I offered the opinion that Lawrence had probably been given a beating, and they were satisfied with that explanation. However, the implication in the film (based on an implication in Lawrence's book *Seven Pillars of Wisdom*) is that Lawrence suffered a humiliating homosexual assault. This is not explicitly depicted in the film, and the historical accuracy of Lawrence's account is likewise in dispute. Unless you are keen on using this scene as some form of teachable moment, you may wish to skirt the issue and simply speculate that something unwelcome and unpleasant happened, which caused Lawrence feelings of shame and disempowerment. (Jose Ferrer was originally reluctant to accept the role of the Turkish Bey because it only represented five minutes of screen time. He later decided those five minutes represented the best work of his career, and Peter O'Toole claimed that working on that scene with Ferrer was better than attending a class in film acting.)

## DECEMBER

### DRAMA

# A Tree Grows in Brooklyn

*1945, 128 minutes, black-and-white*

**Featuring Dorothy McGuire, Peggy Ann Garner, Joan Blondell, James Dunn, Lloyd Nolan.** *Directed by Elia Kazan, written by Frank Davis and Tess Slesinger, based on the novel by Betty Smith*

As the darkest days of the year close around us, many of us turn within and become thoughtful. This is a great time of year for stories of family, human imperfection and the need for redemption. *A Tree Grows in Brooklyn* offers just this kind of story, tender and moving. It centers around young Francie Nolan and her immigrant family, living in Brooklyn in the early years of the 20th century. Like *I Remember Mama*, it is based on a young woman's memoir – this is the east coast version. As with their counterparts in San Francisco, the Nolan family counts out their pennies and dimes on a Saturday. Your children get to see what a free day on the weekend looked like then: taking items to the ragpicker for a return of 9 cents (plus a penny tip), visiting the 5 and 10 Cent Store, trying to get mama to spring for a penny for ice cream, or aiming to read through every book in the library.

This was Elia Kazan's first full-length film. His directorial style seems to have sprung forth fully formed: the clear and evocative storytelling, and the performances so natural that no one seems to be acting at all. His reputation as an actor's director is born out here, and he is already (nine years before he made *On the Waterfront*) working in the realistic style that became so influential in American filmmaking. The world of *A Tree Grows in Brooklyn* was a familiar one for Kazan, as his Greek parents immigrated to New York in 1913 and he grew up in the same environment of struggle balanced with aspiration.

Francie is played by Peggy Ann Garner, in one of the best on-screen performances by a child actor. James Dunn won the Best Supporting Actor Oscar for his turn as Johnny Nolan, the charming ne'er-do-well father Francie adores. Johnny is trying to make a living, using his sweet Irish tenor voice, as a singing waiter. But unfortunately his wages don't always make it home, as one of the traits he brought along from the old country is a fondness for drink. It is hard not to love Johnny, dreamer and poetic soul that he is, but it is impossible to count on him. Dorothy McGuire gives a beautifully complex and understated performance as Katie, the wife who can still be swept away by Johnny's romantic visions (as her daughter is), but then finds herself again on her hands and knees scrubbing the floors, and facing the hard reality of having to be responsible because her husband is not. Joan Blondell brings a bubbly energy to each of her scenes as Sissy, Katie's sister, who seems to have no trouble replacing a disappointing man with a new one – but who calls them all Harry, just to be sure she'll use the right name.

What makes the story so engaging is that these people, these imperfect parents, acknowledge their flaws and want desperately to do better for the sake of their children. Johnny's alcoholism is not condoned, nor is he presented as an abusive father or husband. Only once do we actually see him drunk. He does everything he can to ensure that his daughter will get the education that may lift her out of the poverty of their circumstances. And when he is confronted with his failure to support his family, he sets out to redeem himself as a provider – with tragic results.

It is just as moving when Katie realizes that her struggles have made her hard, that she has favored her son and kept her daughter at arm's length, counting on

> *What makes the story so engaging is that these people, these imperfect parents, acknowledge their flaws and want desperately to do better for the sake of their children.*

Francie to be strong, as the women in her own family are strong. Always a limpidly honest actress, McGuire is especially lovely in the scene where she calls on Francie to help her in childbirth, as there are no grown-up women at hand. One point the movie shows beautifully is the importance of dignity to people who are struggling to hold on to the bottom rung of the ladder. There is a scene in which Katie tries to persuade the doctor who signed the death certificate to record a cause of death that won't shame her children. James Gleason has a lovely scene as McGarrity, the owner of a local bar where Johnny was all too well known. Knowing the family's circumstances, he tries to give Katie some money that he claims was Johnny's. When her pride prevents her from accepting, he offers something she is able to agree to: after-school work for the children. It is bittersweet indeed to find oneself feeling grateful to the man who offers an opportunity for child labor.

Although bittersweet is certainly a strong flavor in *A Tree Grows in Brooklyn*, it is not the only one. There is some laughter (the exchanges between the Nolan children have an appealingly plainspoken quality that anyone familiar with sibling dynamics will enjoy). There is a lot to smile about, not the least being Lloyd Nolan as the young police officer with a courtly manner, who brings hope to the family. And there is the uplifting belief in the power of hope itself, as seen in the little tree that pushes its way up through the shadowy courtyard in a Brooklyn tenement, reaching toward the light.

# DECEMBER
## DRAMA/FANTASY/ROMANCE

# It's a Wonderful Life

*1946, 130 minutes, black-and-white*

**Featuring James Stewart, Donna Reed, Lionel Barrymore, Thomas Mitchell, Henry Travers.** *Directed by Frank Capra, written by Frances Goodrich, Albert Hackett and Frank Capra, based on a story by Philip Van Doren Stern*

If you haven't seen *It's a Wonderful Life*...well, you must have spent every holiday season to date on some other planet. The movie is ubiquitous at this time of year, and for good reason. It's a wonderful film. Many Americans think of Thanksgiving as the kick-off to the holiday season, and this would actually be a great movie to watch before or after consuming too much turkey. It is, after all, about learning to give thanks for the uniqueness of your life. Then again, that makes it a good movie to watch just about any time you need to be reminded about what is truly important.

James Stewart gives an iconic performance as George Bailey, a regular small-town guy. He is the oldest son of the family that runs the Bailey Savings and Loan Association, a company dedicated to the old-fashioned notion that decent, hard-working people should be able to get an affordable mortgage, stay in their homes and build strong neighborhoods and communities. This idea of doing business is considered quaint by the Bailey family's rival Henry Potter, who believes that profit comes first and that real estate is a Darwinian game. Audiences who watched this movie when it first came out might have remembered the steadfast bankers, lawyers, physicians and others who helped their neighbors weather the Great Depression. Contemporary audiences will have new associations with the conflict shown here, between the forces of greed for easy money - and the tenacity and sacrifice it takes to put the welfare of the community first.

George's life is one of ordinary triumphs and ordinary frustrations – but the opening shot of the film, featuring twinkling stars and a celestial conversation, hints to us that George Bailey's life is not to remain ordinary for long. George's greatest dream is to get out of his home town and travel. This desire is repeatedly thwarted by obligations to family, obligations to the business and to the townsfolk it serves. On Christmas Eve one year, after one setback too many, George is finally driven to despair and resolves to end his life by jumping off a bridge. He is saved by a most unlikely-looking angel, Clarence (played by Henry Travers). The rumpled gentleman in the 19th century shirt is actually Clarence Odbody, Angel Second Class, who has been trying to earn his wings for over a hundred years. This is a perfect opportunity for a good deed. However, Clarence does not save George by pulling him out of the river. Instead he jumps into the river first, thus provoking George to do what comes most naturally to him: help someone else.

This is where the not-so-ordinary part of George's life commences. He pulls this quaint-looking older gentleman out of the river and into a world which is governed by his despairing wish: "I wish I'd never been born." It's not a pretty world – it's a harder and more heartbreaking world than it would have been with George in it. His hometown of Bedford Falls is now Pottersville, a nightmare town created by the greed of George's nemesis, wheelchair-bound tycoon Henry Potter (played with all too much relish by Lionel Barrymore, of the legendary acting family. Barrymore was actually confined to a wheelchair in real life at this point, so this fact was exploited for his

> *It has dry humor, offbeat and charming romance, some snappy, fast-paced dialogue, a credible villain and some timeless social issues.*

character). It takes a very cranky George some time to realize what he is seeing, and to fully understand the positive impact his life and his choices have had on all around him.

Since this is a holiday story, George naturally gets to return to his lovely Mary (played by Donna Reed as everyone's ideal wife and mother), and to realize that his life is a great success despite its frustrations. A bell rings on the Christmas tree to signify that somewhere Clarence Odbody has won his wings. As heartwarming as the ending is, the movie is certainly not awash in sentiment or sap. It has dry humor, offbeat and charming romance, some snappy, fast-paced dialogue, a credible villain and some timeless social issues. Plus a reminder that the good one does in one's life does register on the world, and that the most seemingly ordinary life is to be valued.

If you've had enough of Jimmy Stewart for one year (hard to imagine), or if you've simply seen this movie too many times and yet yearn for some homespun American sentiment for the holidays… we can let you off the hook for this year. Allow us to recommend, as an alternate, *Meet Me in St. Louis* (1944), an absolutely charming visit to an American family at the beginning of the last century, on the eve of the World's Fair in St. Louis. The residents of the actual city in Missouri pronounce it St. Lou-is, but you'll have to get used to Judy Garland singing "Meet me in St. Lou-ee, Lou-ee." You will soon forgive her, as she is fetching and fresh, and the movie offers a warmhearted nostalgia we are so often seeking at this season. It's in color (directed with a fine eye by Vincente Minnelli, who married Judy shortly after the film was made and was the father of Liza Minnelli). It's a musical featuring some well-loved songs ("Have Yourself a Merry Little Christmas" and "Clang Clang Clang Went the Trolley" among them), and it features a terrific performance by a young Margaret O'Brien as 'Tootie,' the little sister who doesn't want the family to pack up and move to New York.

# DECEMBER

### DRAMA/FANTASY

# A Christmas Carol

*(shown as* **Scrooge** *in the U.K.)*

*1951, 86 minutes, black-and-white*

**Featuring Alastair Sim, Kathleen Harrison, Mervyn Johns, Hermione Baddeley, Michael Hordern.** *Directed by Brian Desmond-Hurst, adaptation by Noel Langley*

This has got to be the best Christmas movie ever made. Yes, that's a large claim. Every year there are new holiday movies, and countless versions of Charles Dickens' classic tale, *A Christmas Carol*, are amongst the huge numbers of seasonal films available. This version has the feel of being very close to Dickens – the sometimes bleak evocation of the Victorian world, the melodramatic (and highly effective) musical score, the moody black and white cinematography. Yet all of this Dickensian 'feel' takes our attention off the fact that Noel Langley's superb screenplay includes some scenes that are actually not present in the original novella – and that bring great depth and psychological richness to the story.

This adaptation allows us to relate to Ebenezer Scrooge not only when he makes his transformation on Christmas morning – but as we watch his character develop, through many blows and disappointments, from a vulnerable young man to a well-defended recluse, holding human warmth at bay. In this version, Ebenezer is the younger son, and it was his mother's death in giving birth to him that has caused his father to reject him. In the company of the Ghost of Christmas Past, Ebenezer visits the old schoolroom where he spent many a lonely Christmas. He re-experiences the moment when his beloved sister Fan came at last to fetch him home. No matter how adept contemporary film crews are at creating spectacular car crashes, rarely has special effects technology been used with greater impact than in this scene. The grown Ebenezer opens his arms with utter joy at the sight of Fan – only to have her run right through his ghostly figure to embrace his younger self. As the Ghost says, "We are the shadows here," and indeed, Scrooge has made himself like a ghost amongst his fellow men.

Other enhancements seem designed to make the most of an extraordinary ensemble of British actors: Mervyn Johns as the quintessential Bob Cratchit, and Hermione Baddeley as Mrs. Cratchit (she later played the housemaid in *Mary Poppins* and supplied the voice of Madame in the animated *Aristocats*). The role of the housekeeper Mrs. Dilber is beefed up here, so we can enjoy more of the wonderful Cockney flavor of Kathleen Harrison. A character named Mr. Jorkin is added, to give young Ebenezer some help in developing mercenary values: he is gleefully played by Jack Warner. Michael Hordern plays Marley's ghost as a 19th century actor would have – a very, very good 19th century actor – and this is one of the most powerful haunting scenes you will find in any of the versions. The scene of Marley's death is also added to allow Hordern and Alastair Sim, those great old pros, a droll opportunity to show Scrooge's cold-heartedness at its most comically inappropriate. Called to Marley's deathbed, Scrooge is checking his partner's vital signs without the least hint of delicacy or feeling, when Marley opens one doleful eye and fixes it upon him. (One can almost imagine one of the Monty Python crew chirping their famous line, "I'm not dead yet!")

The most indelible performance, in a pitch-perfect cast, is Alastair Sim's as Ebenezer Scrooge. He can integrate into a scene, like Michael Hordern, 19th century theater gestures (falling to his knees, or clutching his head in fear or anguish) which seem completely natural to the character and his world, and never once feel unmotivated or over the top. At the same time, he gives the most

> *The superb screenplay includes some scenes that are actually not present in the original novella – and that bring great depth and psychological richness to the story.*

perfect example of mask and counter-mask you are likely to see in any film. This is when the actor reveals, behind the 'mask' the character presents to the world, the true spirit within - which may be completely the opposite of the surface appearance. In the early scenes in Scrooge's office, Sim dishes out his harshest quips with a twinkle in his eye – almost as though he *enjoys* the permission he has given himself to be so anti-social. It is also the twinkle of the man who, after his sojourn with the spirits, wakes up on Christmas morning full of gratitude to be alive, and declaring "I must stand on my head! I must stand on my head!" Sim is irrepressibly delightful in this scene, capering and chortling and teasing himself and Mrs. Dilber. His true inner spirit has finally burst forth, revealing a man with a great appetite for life, which makes his long isolation the more moving, and his redemption the more joyfully satisfying. One can readily believe that he will have enough life force and vigor to save Tiny Tim, transform the environment around him, and go on to "keep Christmas well" for many years to come. Many fine actors have essayed the role (among them Fredric March, Albert Finney, George C. Scott, Michael Caine, Jack Palance, Patrick Stewart, Frank Langella). Our vote still goes to Alastair Sim as the definitive Scrooge in the definitive 'Christmas Carol.'

**A word of caution:** At all costs, avoid the colorized version of this film. Scenes which are richly evocative in the original just manage to look tatty and cheap with the faked-up color. What appears to be an authentic Victorian office in black and white suddenly looks like a vaudeville stage set in the colorized version. The wonderful mood and atmosphere created in the black and white are entirely sacrificed – it is just not worth it!

## DECEMBER

**MUSICAL/COMEDY/ROMANCE**

# White Christmas

*1954, 120 minutes, color*

**Featuring Bing Crosby, Danny Kaye, Rosemary Clooney, Vera Ellen, Dean Jagger, Mary Wickes.** *Directed by Michael Curtiz; written by Norman Krasna, Norman Panama and Melvin Frank; songs by Irving Berlin*

We began the year in color, enjoying the comic and musical talents of Danny Kaye – and that seems as good a way as any to finish up the year as well! Especially since *White Christmas* also features terrific songs by the unbeatable Irving Berlin, crooned by Bing Crosby and Rosemary Clooney (who was famous for being Rosemary Clooney long before she became famous for being George Clooney's aunt), and surrounded by a warm-hearted story. There is an earlier black and white version with a related story, Berlin songs and a pairing of Bing Crosby and Fred Astaire as a performing act (the one is more of a singer, the other more of a dancer). *Holiday Inn* (1942) is a terrific movie too, and highly recommended – if you're still full of holiday spirit, why not watch both?

Both movies make use of a device common in the early film musicals. The main characters are entertainers, and that gives them constant (and natural) excuses to sing, dance and crack wise. In *White Christmas*, Danny Kaye and Bing Crosby team up as soldiers, entertaining the troops on Christmas Eve near the enemy lines in Europe during World War Two. Bing Crosby's character is Bob Wallace, already a successful performer back home; Danny Kaye's Phil Davis insinuates his way into the act and they return from the war as Wallace and Davis, Broadway song-and-dance duo, then successful producers. One is more of a singer (Bing Crosby, who else?) and the other more of a dancer (and physical comedian – Danny Kaye, naturally). Or as Kaye says when Crosby attempts a wisecrack, "Ha ha, the crooner becoming the clown…"

Their partnership is a little too successful, it turns out, as they find themselves working night and day – once they close a show in Florida, their holiday "break" involves going to New York to get the next one ready. Danny Kaye embarks on a campaign to get Bing Crosby to fall in love and get married, so they can have a few moments apart each day. This is, of course, where Rosemary Clooney and Vera Ellen come in, as Betty and Judy Haynes, a pair of performers who have a sister act they want to try out for the famous producers Wallace and Davis. One is more of a singer (Clooney) and the other is more of a dancer (Vera Ellen). Their routine, "Sisters, Sisters," performed in matching blue dresses with big blue feather fans, is charming and funny. Even funnier is the same routine performed later in the evening by Wallace and Davis in drag while the women, who can't afford the rent at their boarding house, slip out the window of their dressing room and head for the train. (In between these two numbers is a show-stopping romantic dance, as Danny Kaye and Vera Ellen get to know one another to "The Best Things Happen While You're Dancing.")

The pair of duos wind up on the train together, and find themselves bound for an inn in Vermont, where the girls have their next booking. It happens to be run by none other than General Waverly, Wallace and Davis's beloved commanding officer during the war, now retired as an innkeeper. Not a successful innkeeper, unfortunately. Vermont is unseasonably warm this particular season – and no snow means no guests, and no show for Betty and Judy. Wallace and Davis set out to solve everyone's problems by putting on a show at the inn to attract customers, a Wallace and Davis extravaganza. Many production numbers are thereby introduced (including a wonderful satire of the modern dance of the

> *Holiday Inn is a terrific movie too, and highly recommended – if you're still full of holiday spirit, why not watch both?*

time, performed by Danny Kaye and choreographed by an uncredited Bob Fosse). Wallace and Betty fall for one another, and we get to enjoy Crosby and Clooney by the fireside crooning "Count Your Blessings" to one another. Romantic complications ensue.

Irving Berlin was an ardent American patriot and, although he never wore uniform himself, he was a big fan of the Army. A sentimental plot unfolds, in which Wallace and Davis conspire to honor General Waverly (played with wry warmth by Dean Jagger). And, of course, right on cue….it snows! If you don't happen to like the songs celebrating the joys of being in the army, you can still enjoy a smile about the fact that the iconic holiday song "White Christmas" was penned by a Jewish songwriter… born Israel Bailine.

### TRICKY BIT:

One of the numbers in the show that's being prepared for the inn is an homage to old minstrel shows, although fortunately no one actually dons blackface. It's actually an opportunity, if you wish, to talk to kids about how characters and jokes that are considered perfectly innocent at one point in history can wind up looking very different through the eyes of another time and consciousness. The number mainly features some of the corny old "Mr. Bones" joke routines that were used in actual minstrel shows – and then mercifully moves on to some spectacular dancing by Vera Ellen with her million-dollar legs.

Is *White Christmas* as light and easily digested as snowflakes on your tongue? Sure. Is *Holiday Inn*, the earlier Fred Astaire-Bing Crosby version more revered by critics? Yes. (And once again, it is well worth viewing!) But corny as the movie may seem at times, we urge you to surrender. Enjoy the lavish and colorful costumes by legendary designer Edith Head (later parodied as the diva costumer Edna Mode, in Brad Bird's brilliant animated film *The Incredibles*). And hum along to the songs by one of the greatest tune-meisters of the 20th century. It may yet become an annual event in your house, and you all may find yourselves dreaming of *White Christmas*.

# acknowledgments

Of course, I can never thank enough all the artists and technicians who created these fabulous movies – except, perhaps, by writing another book urging you to see more of their work. But I can thank Richard T. Jameson, film critic extraordinaire, who read and commented upon this manuscript in its entirety. His sharp eye caught many inaccuracies – any that may have slipped through are entirely my responsibility, not his. I am grateful also for the comments of film aficionados Robert Cumbow, Frank Corrado, Roger Downey, David Vaughan, and Stephanie F. Ogle of Cinema Books in Seattle.

Valuable editorial feedback on early drafts was provided by Ruth Neuwald Falcon, Betsy Goldberg, Charles Fleming and Leisa Goldberg, and also words of wisdom from Liam Lavery. Mandy Dumins made an important contribution to the initial design of the book. Tom Robbins, Mark Pearson, Charles Harrington Elster and Donna Shanley offered sage professional advice. I am grateful to Michael Matisse for his encouragement, and his invaluable help with the visuals. And to Craig Wilson, Frank Dauer and Kory Kapitke, for both emotional and practical support.

The layout wizard is John Engerman of Bicameral Design, and the charming cover art is by illustrator Karen Lewis.

This book would never have happened in the first place if it were not for my husband Arne Zaslove, whose cries of "What do you mean...?" inspired not only the title but also the idea. His love of film, of artists, of creativity wherever it is found, is a nurturing source for anyone who knows him. He has shepherded this version through production, after untold months of feeding the author and holding her hand.

Warmest thanks of all go to our son and daughter, Max and Jesse, who have embraced this project and been the final arbiters on every selection. Watching these movies together has enriched our family time immeasurably. With these two incredible young people to share our lives and our passions, Arne and I could not possibly be more blessed.

*"If you know all these great movies and famous stars – why not share?"*
Jesse, age 8, to a friend's mother

# coming attractions

Did you enjoy your first year of classic movies? Is your family hooked?
Well, there are plenty more classic films to enjoy!

Watch for these upcoming guides…

### ▶ Volume 2: What Do You Mean You Haven't Seen…? Classics of Foreign Film

This is for adults, not families. Create your own film club, modeled on your book club…only less reading to do! Plan to meet every 2 weeks, and catch up on the greatest must-see classics by Bergman, Fellini, Kurosawa, Antonioni, Eisenstein, Truffaut – 25 of the foreign films you must see, before you can appreciate the contemporary crop of foreign films. (Not to mention before you can sip a latte with Woody Allen, and hold your own in a conversation about the great works of cinema….)

### ▶ Volume 3: What Do You Mean You Haven't Seen…? Build Your Own Film Festival

Once your family has identified the actors and genres you like, dig deeper into them! Create your own mini- film festival at home for:

| | |
|---|---|
| **Musicals** | Check out the versatility of: |
| **Westerns** | |
| **Drama and Epic** | **Audrey Hepburn** |
| **Suspense and Film Noir** | **Katharine Hepburn / Spencer Tracy** |
| **The Great Clowns** | **Humphrey Bogart** |
| **Screwball / Comedy** | **Ingrid Bergman** |
| **Animated** | **Cary Grant** |
| **Shakespeare / Historical** | **James Stewart** |
| *and more……* | **Marlon Brando** |
| | **James Cagney** |
| | *and more…..* |

Hold your own Academy Awards ceremony and let each member of the family 'Academy' vote on favorite performers and genres.

### ▶ Volume 4: What Do You Mean You Haven't Seen…? Chick Flicks

Movies to see with your daughter, mother, sister, best friend or cousin…… Need we say more?

### ▶ Volume 5: What Do You Mean You Haven't Seen…? Family Favorites: 1968 – 2008

Our candidates for the films that will become classics in the 21st century… that have the same spirit, energy and talent we find in the great classics of American film. Get to know Jackie Chan, Johnny Depp, Alan Arkin… Classics didn't stop getting made when the ratings system came into use. But parents did start looking for the G or PG rating, without always knowing whether a movie was a keeper… Let us remind you of some of the great movies made in the last 40 years, and why they're great!

www.ingramcontent.com/pod-product-compliance
Lightning Source LLC
Chambersburg PA
CBHW042008150426
43195CB00002B/59